Gems

Questions and Answers books are available on the following subjects

QUESTIONS & ANSWERS

Gems

P. G. Read

Newnes Technical Books

Newnes Technical Books
is an imprint of the Butterworth Group
which has principal offices in
London, Sydney, Toronto, Wellington, Durban and Boston

First published 1981

British Library Cataloguing in Publication Data

Read, P G
  Gems. – (Questions & answers).
  1. Precious stones
  I. Title   II. Series
  549   QE392

  ISBN 0-408-00546-7

Photoset by Butterworths Litho Preparation Department
Printed in England by Butler & Tanner Ltd, Frome, Somerset

Preface

This book has been written to provide answers to typical questions which I am asked when giving talks on gemstones and related subjects. Gemmology itself is a relatively new science, and is unusual in that it overlaps into many other related sciences such as mineralogy, geology, physics and chemistry. Despite this wide scientific base, gemmology is a very practical subject which developed originally to serve the needs of the jewellery trade. Today, however, many people have become involved in the study of gemstones because of an interest in both collecting and identifying gem materials.

For those who are interested simply in knowing more about the gems in their jewellery, and for the amateur lapidary who needs to be aware of the physical and optical properties of the material he is polishing, this book can provide a starting point. For students of gemmology, and in particular for those who are taking courses leading to the Fellowship Diploma of the Gemmological Association of Great Britain, I recommend my earlier work *Beginner's Guide to Gemmology* which is also published by Newnes Technical Books.

P. G. R.

Contents

1
The science of gemstones

What is gemmology?

Gemmology is the science of gem materials, and covers all aspects of where and how they occur in the earth, their physical and optical properties and characteristics, the techniques used in their cutting and polishing and the instruments and methods employed in their identification.

What is meant by a 'gem material'?

This is any material, including organic and inorganic substances, which is suitable for use in a piece of jewellery.

What makes a gem material suitable for use in jewellery?

There are three basic qualities which need to be present in some degree in all gem materials. The most obvious of these is *beauty*. In coloured gems, the depth and purity of colour may be the prime factors, while in a colourless gem beauty may depend on the stone's brilliance and freedom from flaws.

The second quality necessary in a gemstone is *rarity*, although this is a more variable factor, and one which is affected by both supply and demand. A faceted piece of coloured glass (known as 'paste') may be beautiful, but because it can be mass-produced it cannot be considered to be rare. Amethyst is an example of the effect of rarity on the value of a gem, as this was once a relatively rare and costly stone until the discovery of the large Brazilian deposits in the eighteenth century. Today the balance between supply and demand for amethyst is changing again as sources of good-quality material are becoming depleted. As a result of this the value of the gem is rising.

The third and perhaps the most practical quality necessary in a gem which is to be mounted in a piece of jewellery is *hardness* or *durability*. Quite apart from the knocks experienced by gems in everyday use, they are also subjected to the abrasive action of dust which contains minute particles of quartz (a major constituent in the earth's crust). If the gem is softer than the quartz particles, these will in time reduce its surface polish to a dull matt finish.

Not every gem possesses all three qualities of beauty, rarity and durability in the same degree. Diamond, ruby and sapphire are the main exceptions, all three of these stones having beauty, rarity and exceptional durability. With diamond, rarity is maintained (despite the enormous quantities mined – over 14 million carats of gem quality in 1980!) by the high demand for this gem. With other stones there is some compromise in the balance of the three qualities; opal for instance is valued as a gem by virtue of its beauty and relative rarity, despite its softness and porosity.

What is the difference between an organic and an inorganic gem?

An organic gem is one which is derived from a once-living organism. Examples of organic gem materials are amber, ivory, bone, jet, coral, pearl and tortoiseshell. In contrast to this, inorganic gems (with the exception of the man-made varieties) were produced in the earth's crust as a result of the forces and processes of inorganic (i.e. non-living) nature.

The majority of these inorganic gemstones are minerals, which means that they are mined from the earth in a reasonably high state of purity, and therefore have a chemical composition and physical characteristics which are uniform throughout their bulk.

There are well over 2000 different mineral species which have been recovered from the earth's crust, but only about 50 of these have the necessary qualities of beauty, rarity and durability to be used as gemstones in jewellery. Of these 50 gem materials, perhaps only 10 are ever seen regularly in the window of a jeweller's shop.

While minerals are relatively pure chemical compounds, the bulk of the earth's crust is made up from mixtures of minerals, and these mixtures are called rocks. Granite, for example, is a very common rock in the earth's surface and is composed of a mixture of feldspar, quartz and mica. Although the majority of gemstones are minerals, the expensive blue lapis lazuli stone is a mixture of azurite, sodalite, calcite and pyrite, and is therefore more accurately described as a gem rock rather than a gem mineral.

Do gems differ very much from each other in composition and characteristics?

Yes they do, and this is fortunate for the jeweller and gemmologist who often have to use these differences to identify a gem. A gemstone's basic identifying features are its optical properties (refractive index and double refraction) and its physical characteristics (hardness and specific gravity). These are called the gemstone's *constants*, and are generally quite specific and unvarying for each gem material (a table showing these constants is given in Appendix 2 of this book).

Descriptions of all these properties and characteristics appear in Chapters 3 and 5, together with details of the instruments used in their measurement. In addition, Appendix 3 gives the characteristics and occurrence of the more important gem materials.

Why do some gemstones have more than one name?

This usually happens when a particular gem mineral *species* has a number of different *varieties*, all of which have their own

3

Table 1. Examples of gemstone species and variety names

Species	Variety
Beryl	Emerald, aquamarine, morganite (pink), heliodor (yellow), goshenite (colourless)
Chrysoberyl	Chrysoberyl (yellow, greenish-yellow), alexandrite (red in tungsten light, green in daylight), cymophane (greenish-yellow cat's eye)
Corundum	Ruby, sapphire (blue, violet, green, yellow, pink, orange, colourless)
Orthoclase feldspar	Moonstone, orthoclase (yellow)
Microcline feldspar	Amazonite (green)
Plagioclase feldspar	Oligoclase (yellow), labradorite (multi-coloured sheen), sunstone (bronze-spangled), aventurine (green, spangled), albite moonstone
Almandine garnet	(purple/red)
Pyrope garnet	(blood red)
Grossular garnet	Hessonite (orange/brown, green and pink), massive grossular (jade green)
Andradite garnet	Demantoid (green), topazolite (golden yellow)
Spessartite garnet	(orange, yellow, flame red)
Uvarovite garnet	(emerald green)
Opal	White opal, black opal, water opal (colourless with internal iridescence), Mexican fire opal (orange), green opal
Quartz	Amethyst, citrine (yellow), rose quartz, smoky quartz, rock crystal (colourless), aventurine quartz (green, blue or brown with mica spangles), tiger's eye (yellow/brown), hawk's eye (blue/green), jasper (red/brown)
Chalcedony (cryptocrystalline quartz)	Chalcedony (blue/grey unbanded), agate (curved concentric bands), cornelian (red/orange), chrysoprase (green), onyx (straight bands)
Tourmaline	Achroite (colourless), indicolite (blue), shorl (black), tourmaline (green, yellow, pink, red, brown)

identifying names. For instance, ruby and sapphire are the colour variety names for the gem mineral species corundum. Similarly, quartz is the species name, and rock crystal, citrine, amethyst and smoky quartz are all varieties of quartz (*Table 1*).

It sometimes happens that a gem species also has alternative names, such as iolite/cordierite/dichroite (which are all the same gem material), and zoisite/tanzanite (the latter being derived from Tanzania, the source of the gemstone). Some of these alternative names are the preferred ones used in mineralogy as distinct from gemmology (e.g. fluorite and fluorspar), but sometimes names such as rubellite (for pink tourmaline) and water sapphire (for iolite) appear to have been coined with the intent of misleading the purchaser, and their use is being discouraged.

What is meant by the terms 'precious' and 'semi-precious'?

These terms were used originally to separate gemstones into two valuation groups. Precious gems included the most valuable stones such as diamond, ruby, sapphire and emerald. All the remaining stones were classified as semi-precious. Today the use of these arbitrary terms is being discouraged, and all gems are individually assessed by virtue of their beauty, rarity and durability.

How were gemstones formed in the earth's crust?

As the primeval earth cooled, and its outer crust began to solidify, gemstones, like other minerals, slowly crystallised either out of the molten rock magma, or from chemically-rich aqueous solutions.

Gemstones such as moonstone, quartz (i.e. rock crystal, citrine, amethyst), tourmaline, aquamarine, topaz and zircon grew as crystals either from aqueous or molten chemical residues, the quartz varieties sometimes becoming trapped in rock cavities to form the spherical crystalline chambers called *geodes*.

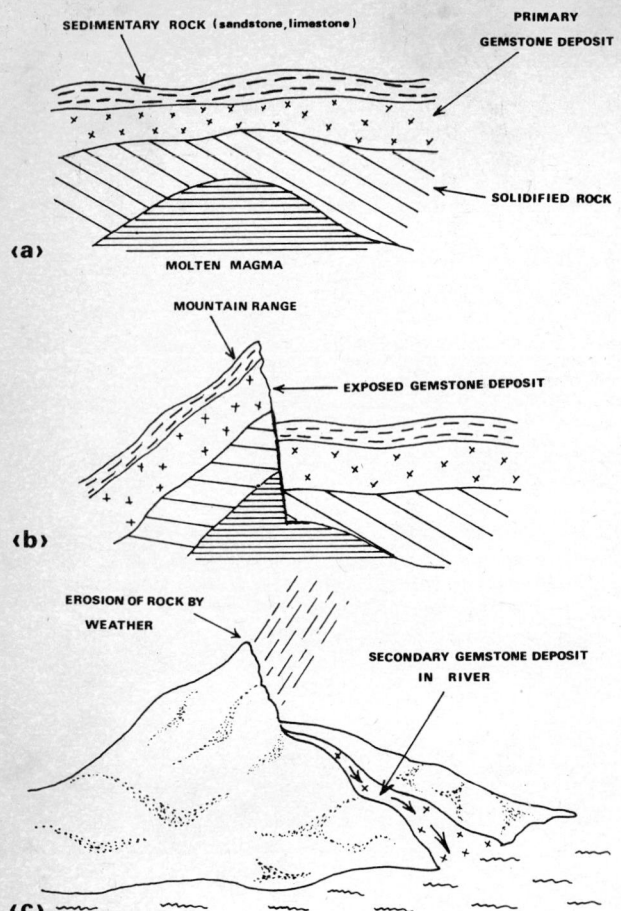

Fig. 1. (a) Formation of a primary gemstone deposit, (b) its subsequent exposure due to rock upheaval, and (c) the formation of a secondary gemstone deposit

6

Gemstones such as emerald, alexandrite, ruby and sapphire were often the result of chemical reactions occurring as molten rocks forced their way into crevices in cooler rocks. Earth movements which produced the shearing and crushing of rocks resulted in the production of garnet, andalusite, serpentine and jade.

With the exception of diamond, all of these gemstone formations took place in the topmost strata of the earth's crust millions of years ago, and for this reason gem minerals can justly be classified as the true antiques of the jewellery world!

Further upheavals in the earth's crust exposed many of the gem-bearing rocks (*Fig. 1*), and the action of the weather eventually loosened the gems which were then carried away by rivers to form the present-day gem gravels of Sri Lanka, Burma and Thailand. These water-borne gems are known as *alluvial* or *secondary* deposits.

Was diamond formed in the same way?

No, diamond is unique in that it crystallised much deeper in the earth's crust than all other gemstones. Because of our knowledge of the conditions necessary to synthesise *industrial* diamonds, the current theory is that diamonds crystallised from graphite (or even from carbon dioxide gas) at a depth of between 100 and 150 miles beneath the earth's surface. At these great depths, the necessary temperature and pressure conditions existed which enabled the carbon atoms to be forced into the tight symmetrical pattern of the diamond crystal.

These diamond crystals were then thought to have been carried to the surface of the earth by gigantic explosions of gas which forced the molten diamond-bearing rocks up through flaws and cracks in the earth's crust in a volcanic-like eruption. The molten rocks then cooled and solidified to form the present-day diamond *pipes*, which are the *primary* source of all diamonds. Over millions of years, the tops of these pipes were eroded away by weathering action, and the diamonds in them washed into rivers and distributed along marine terraces to form the world's *secondary* diamond deposits.

Are there diamonds in all volcanic pipes?

Only about 0.01% of all known pipes have diamonds in them. The reason for this, even in diamond-rich areas like Kimberley in South Africa, is that diamonds only survived their long journey to the surface of the earth if the pressure and temperature of the surrounding rock dropped in a manner which maintained the carbon in its crystalline form. If the pressure dropped too quickly, as was generally the case, the diamonds burned up and reverted back to non-crystalline carbon or carbon dioxide gas.

Why are diamonds more expensive than most other gems?

This is partly because of the high cost of mining them, and partly due to the cost of cutting and polishing a material which is the hardest of all the gem minerals. However, some of the very rare gemstones, such as alexandrite (which changes its colour appearance from green in daylight to red in tungsten light), and top quality rubies and emeralds, are more costly than even the top value ice-white diamonds.

Most diamonds contain a yellow tint, and are described as belonging to the 'Cape Series' because of this. The greater the degree of this yellowness, the less valuable is the stone. To complete the picture, the rare coloured diamonds, known as 'fancies', are often up to three times the price of colourless diamonds. These fancy coloured diamonds occur in attractive hues of canary yellow, pink, green and blue.

How are gemstones mined?

This varies enormously with the type of gemstone. Opal, for instance, is a secondary deposit, and was washed out of silica-bearing rocks and soils to solidify as thin veins of crystallised silica gel in the cracks and fissures of the underlying sandstone. In Australia (the main source of precious opal), small pits are sunk to reach the opal layers, which occur at depths from between 5 and 50 feet beneath the surface.

In Sri Lanka, Burma and Thailand, the gem-rich gravels lie in broad strata, usually along the courses of ancient river beds. These are reached by sinking rectangular pits, often to a depth of 20–30 feet. Once the topsoil or overburden is removed, the gravels are hauled out and dumped in a compound.

When sufficient gravels have been stockpiled in this manner, they are scooped into hemispherical woven baskets and washed in a nearby pool. The washing motion filters out the silt and sand through the open weave of the basket and the lighter materials are spun out over its edge. This leaves the heavier gem gravels concentrated in the bottom of the basket. These are then tipped out and hand-sorted.

Emerald mining in Colombia consists of cutting a series of 'steps' or terraces in the hillside to reach the emerald crystals which occur in veins and cavities in beds of shale.

Diamond mining at a primary or pipe deposit usually starts as an open-cast operation, bulldozers being used to scoop up the diamond-bearing kimberlite rock and load it into dumper trucks, which then transport it to the crushing and separating plant. When the open-cast mine reaches a certain depth, it becomes uneconomic to continue mining in this way. A shaft is then sunk alongside the pipe and horizontal tunnels are cut through the pipe to extract the kimberlite rock.

In Sierra Leone, the diamond deposits are mainly alluvial, and the diamonds are recovered from the banks and beds of rivers in a manner similar to that used when 'panning' for gold.

Along the coastline of the Namib desert in South West Africa, diamonds are recovered from beneath the sands. Inland from the shoreline, up to 30 feet of sand overburden is stripped away to gain access to the diamond-rich gravels on the underlying ancient marine terraces. A similar operation is carried out beyond the shoreline by building temporary dikes to hold back the sea.

2
Colour in gemstones

What is the cause of colour in gemstones?

Colour in a gemstone is produced as the result of the absorption by the stone of certain colours in the white light passing through it, or reflected back from its surface. White light is composed of a

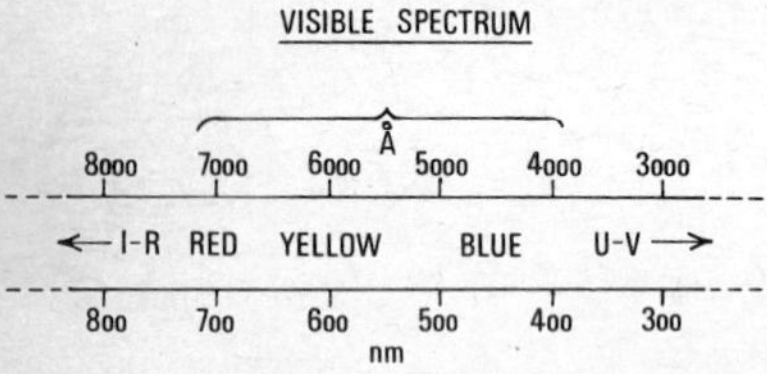

VISIBLE SPECTRUM

Fig. 2. *The visible spectrum is bounded at one end by invisible infra-red (I.-R.) rays, and at the other end by ultra-violet (U.-V.) rays. Wavelengths of the spectral colours are shown in both Ångström units (Å) and nanometres (nm). There are 10 Ångströms to the nanometre, and 1 million nanometres to the millimetre*

roughly equal mixture of all the colours in the visible spectrum (*Fig. 2*) and when a part of this spectrum is absorbed by the gem, the resulting colour is due to the combined effect of the remaining parts of the spectrum.

For example, if the blue/violet end of the spectrum is absorbed by a gemstone (*Fig. 3a*) it will appear as a yellow stone (because

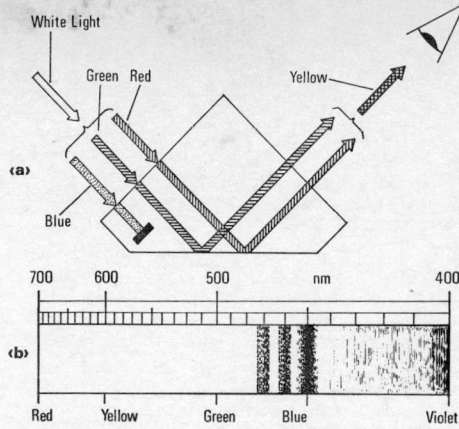

Fig. 3. (a) Absorption of the blue component in white light makes the gemstone appear yellow. (b) The typical absorption spectrum seen with sapphire; the three bands in the blue indicate the presence of iron

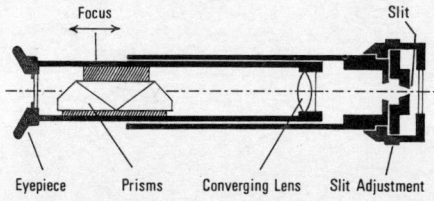

Fig. 4. Construction of a prism-type spectroscope. The compound prism on the left disperses the light entering the instrument into its spectral colours

of this, yellow is described as being the *complementary* colour to violet).

The process by which a gemstone filters out part of the visible spectrum is called *selective absorption*. The absorbed sections of the white light can be made visible by using an instrument called a *spectroscope* (*Fig. 4*). This takes the light which has passed through the gemstone (or, in the case of an opaque stone, reflected from its surface) and spreads it out into a continuous spectrum of colour from red to violet. The absorbed or missing parts of the white light can then be detected as vertical dark bands or lines across the spectrum. The overall result as viewed through the spectroscope is called an *absorption spectrum* (*Fig. 3b*).

Colour can also be caused by the effects of *sheen* and *dispersion*. These are two optical effects which are dealt with under 'Optical properties of gemstones' in Chapter 5.

What causes a gemstone to absorb parts of the spectrum?

There are two basic causes of selective absorption in gemstones, both of which are fundamentally related. The first and most common of these is due to the presence in the gemstone of one or more of eight metallic *transition* elements. These are *titanium, vanadium, chromium, manganese, iron, nickel, cobalt* and *copper*. Examples of gemstones coloured by the transition elements are given in *Table 2*.

The colour effect produced by these transition elements varies from gemstone to gemstone. For example, in corundum, chromium produces the red hues of ruby, while in beryl it gives rise to the green of emerald. Iron is a relatively common element in the earth and is responsible for the colours seen in peridot, aquamarine, blue and green tourmaline and several of the garnets. It is also present in varying degrees in sapphire, even in the popular blue variety where the dominant colouring element is titanium.

It must be mentioned that there are two ways in which a transition element can be present in a gemstone. The first of these occurs when it forms a part of the gemstone's chemical structure. Examples of this can be seen in malachite (containing copper) and rhodonite (containing manganese). The second way occurs when the transition element is present as an impurity, and this happens in the majority of gemstones (e.g. ruby, sapphire, citrine, amethyst, topaz, aquamarine, emerald, etc.).

Table 2. Some gemstones which are coloured by transition elements

Transition element	Gemstone
Titanium	Blue sapphire, benitoite
Vanadium	Blue zoisite, green vanadium beryl, alexandrite simulant (synthetic corundum), violet sapphire
Chromium	Ruby, emerald, alexandrite, red spinel, pyrope garnet, chrome grossular garnet, demantoid garnet, chrome diopside, jadeite, pink topaz
Manganese	Rhodonite, rhodochrosite, spessartite, rose quartz
Iron	Sapphire, sinhalite, peridot, aquamarine, tourmaline, enstatite, amethyst, almandine
Nickel	Chrysoprase, synthetic green and yellow sapphires, green opal
Cobalt	Synthetic blue spinel, blue synthetic quartz, cobalt glass
Copper	Malachite, dioptase, turquoise, synthetic green sapphire

Gemstones which owe their colour to their own chemical composition are called *idiochromatic* (i.e. 'self-coloured') gems, while those which are coloured by impurities are called *allochromatic* (i.e. 'other coloured') gems.

Because they owe their colour to impurities, allochromatic gems (which in their completely pure state occur as colourless stones) can be difficult to identify by colour alone, and for a positive classification it becomes necessary to measure their optical and physical constants.

13

The second and less common colouring 'mechanism' is the presence of crystal defects or damage within the stone. The two principal gemstones which owe their colour not to the presence of transition elements, but to crystal defects, are zircon and diamond.

In coloured zircons, these defects were produced by nuclear bombardment from once radioactive uranium and thorium atoms present in the gemstone. In diamond, the yellow, green and brown tints are the result of crystal defects caused by nitrogen atoms replacing carbon atoms in the crystalline lattice. Blue diamonds also owe their colour to crystal defects, which in this case are caused by the replacement of carbon atoms by atoms of boron. Even the rare fancy coloured diamonds are thought to be coloured by defects produced by a combination of nitrogen, boron and the effects of natural nuclear irradiation within the earth.

Can the absorption spectra seen in gemstones be used to identify the colouring element?

Yes, the number, grouping and positions of absorption bands can often indicate the element or elements responsible for a gemstone's colour. However, because the absorption spectra produced by the transition elements are modified by the 'host' crystal, they are often distinctive enough to provide positive identification of the gemstone itself. For this reason, most books on gem testing (see Appendix 1) include representative pictures of gemstone spectra.

Are there any other chemicals which can colour a gemstone?

There are a group of chemicals called the *rare earths* which are often used to produce colour in man-made gems such as yttrium aluminium garnet (YAG) and cubic zirconium oxide (zirconia). When viewed through a spectroscope, these elements produce very prominent and distinctive absorption lines known as *fine line spectra*. The rare earths used to colour man-made gems include didymium, erbium, dysprosium, holium, thulium and cerium. They very occasionally appear in natural gemstones (e.g. didymium in yellow apatite), and when present, the resulting spectral lines are much weaker in intensity. If the lines are spread fairly evenly across the spectrum they have little overall effect on the gem's colour.

Why does a gemstone such as alexandrite appear as one colour in daylight and a different colour in tungsten light?

When this effect occurs, it is usually due to the presence of chromic oxide as a colouring impurity. In alexandrite this results in a broad central absorption band in the yellow part of the spectrum which causes the stone to appear red in the blue-deficient light of a tungsten lamp (or candle light), and green in the more evenly balanced spectrum of daylight.

Can the colour of gemstones be improved or changed artificially?

Yes, some gemstones such as agate and jade have slightly porous surfaces and can be stained to improve their colour. This is not a legitimate process as it is not permanent, and can be easily removed. However, several of the coloured gemstones seen in a jeweller's shop window are the products of permanent colour change or colour improvement processes. Because these processes result in a permanent and irreversible colour change they are accepted as a legitimate practice.

How do these processes work?

The theory behind many of the artificially induced colour processes is complex, and even today is not fully understood. With the majority of gemstones these processes are based on heat treatment, although some stones are improved in colour by exposure to radioactive isotopes and X-rays.

In gems whose colour is deepened or made less attractive by the presence of an iron compound, this colouring element is probably driven out of the stone by the heat treatment.

With zircon, whose colours are mainly due to crystal defects, the heating probably allows the crystal structure to partially 'repair' or 'heal' itself.

What are the temperatures used in the heat treatment of gemstones?

Brown and yellow topaz can be turned pink by heating it to 500–600°C. If it is heated above 600°C it becomes colourless. The popular shade of blue in zircon is produced by heating brown stones to 900–1000°C in an atmosphere deficient in oxygen. If the same stones are heated in air to 850–900°C, they either change to a golden brown or become colourless.

Can diamonds also be artificially coloured?

Yes, but in general this is a more complex process. There are two main reasons for artificially colouring a diamond; one of these is to improve, or even lighten, the colour of a yellow stone, and the second one is to turn an unattractively coloured stone into a fancy coloured (and therefore more valuable) diamond.

Before the more exotic present-day methods of diamond coloration were available, many yellow stones had their colour 'improved' by placing a spot of blue dye on the rear facets of the gem. Because the yellowness of the diamond is the result of its absorption of light at the violet end of the spectrum, the blue dye had the effect of 'cancelling out' the yellowness in the stone and making it appear more white (this is the reason why yellowish diamonds which have a blue fluorescence appear to be whiter when viewed under daylight conditions).

A later technique, based on the same principle, involved coating the rear facets of the diamond with the type of bluish fluoride which is used as an anti-reflection coating on camera lenses.

The modern technique of colouring diamond uses a source of nuclear radiation to produce 'defects' in the crystal's lattice structure, and this is followed by heat treatment to bring about the required colour change.

Low-energy atomic particles, as developed by an electron accelerator, or a cyclotron, result in a colour change which is only skin deep. With this process, which is the method gaining favour in the USA, any errors in colour change can be rectified by repolishing the diamond's facets and starting again.

Colour changes can also be induced by irradiating the diamond with high-energy neutrons in an atomic reactor, and then heat treating the stone. This results in a colour change which penetrates the whole body of the diamond.

With all these irradiation-type colour change processes, the resulting colour, although more pleasing in hue, is never lighter than the diamond's original natural colour. More recently, however, experiments in the research laboratories of the American General Electric Company have shown that the yellow tints of Cape Series diamonds can be lightened by a high-temperature/high-pressure annealing process.

Is it possible to detect that gemstones have been artificially coloured?

With dyed or stained gems the colour can usually be detected by its effect on the stone's absorption spectrum. With the heat treatment processes, however, it is almost impossible to detect colour improvement, although the latest research work indicates that an unusually high level of fluorescence coupled with subtle changes in the appearance of a gem's inclusions (these are small particles and flaws within the stone) may provide proof of heat treatment.

With fancy coloured diamonds it is often very important from a valuation point of view to be able to decide whether the colour is natural, or whether it has been induced by nuclear irradiation followed by heat treatment. Inspection of the stone sometimes provides clues, but the most positive proof is usually obtained by the use of the spectroscope, which in treated stones reveals either a narrow diagnostic absorption band in the deep yellow, or faint signs of the absorption bands which caused the diamond's original colour together with bands responsible for the new colour.

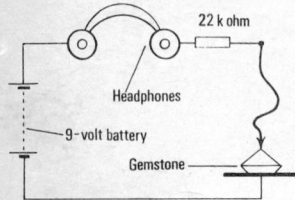

Fig. 5. *A simple test circuit for checking the electrical conductivity of blue diamonds. Because it is able to pass an electric current, a natural blue diamond will produce a scratching sound in the headphones when the test probe is moved over its surface*

Natural blue diamonds owe their colour to the presence within the crystal of boron atoms, and these make the stones partially conductive to an electric current. Blue diamonds produced by nuclear irradiation do not possess this property, and can be distinguished from naturally-coloured stones by checking their electrical conductivity (*Fig. 5*).

3
Gemstone chemistry and related physical properties

What are gemstones composed of?

Apart from diamond, which is unique among gems because it consists entirely of a single element, carbon, gemstones are chemical combinations or *compounds* of various chemical elements, the commonest of these being oxygen and silica.

Is there a connection between the chemical composition and the durability of a gem?

A broad relationship does exist, although in the case of gem minerals the stone's crystalline structure also plays an important part. One of the main reasons for diamond's hardness is the simplicity and compactness of its crystal structure.

The chemical composition of the majority of gemstones can be related to their durability as follows:

Oxides. These are the result of a chemical combination between a metal and oxygen. Gems produced in this way are usually hard and resistant to acid attack. Examples are chrysoberyl ($BeAl_2O_4$), corundum (i.e. ruby and sapphire – Al_2O_3), quartz (i.e. amethyst, citrine, etc. – SiO_2), and spinel ($MgAl_2O_4$).

Carbonates. These are formed by the combination of a metal and carbonic acid. Carbonate gems are invariably soft and are easily attacked by acids. Examples are malachite ($Cu(OH)_2CuCO_3$) and rhodochrosite ($MnCO_3$).

Phosphates. These are compounds of a metal with phosphoric acid. Like the carbonates they are soft and not very resistant to acid attack. Examples of phosphate gems are apatite (Ca_5F,ClP_3O_{12}) and turquoise (a complex compound of phosphorus, water, copper and aluminium).

Silicates. These represent the majority of gemstones, and are compounds of silicic acid and a metal. Silicate gems are hard and very durable. Examples are beryl (i.e. emerald and aquamarine), garnet (a group of gems comprising silicates of magnesium, manganese, iron, calcium, aluminium and chromium in various combinations), peridot $(Mg_2Fe_2SiO_4)$ and zircon $(ZrSiO_4)$.

How is the durability or hardness of a gem assessed?

An impression of the hardness of a gemstone can often be obtained simply by inspecting its polished surface through a hand lens. In the case of a faceted stone, the flatness of the facets and the 'sharpness' of the facet edges will provide a good indication of hardness. With the softer gem materials, the facet edges will tend to be rounded, but with diamond they will be sharp and well defined.

With mounted gemstones that have been worn in jewellery for some years, the condition of the facet surfaces and edges will also provide clues about the hardness of the gem. The relative softness of glass imitation gems can be seen in the number of scratches on their facets and in the damaged condition of their facet edges. In contrast to this, a ruby or sapphire will show far less damage, and a diamond, even a family heirloom that is hundreds of years old, will still be in prime condition.

How is the hardness of a gem tested?

A comparative hardness test using the *Mohs* hardness scale can be used to check the hardness of a gemstone. In its basic form this test depends upon the production of a scratch on the surface of the gemstone, and for this reason is only used when other tests have failed to identify the gem. When the scratch test is used, it is best confined to the smallest possible mark on the underside of the gem in the immediate area of its girdle or circumference (a scratch made on the top, or further down the rear facets, will be much more visible).

In the Mohs scale of hardness, 10 materials are used as hardness standards. Starting with the softest standard at 1 and ending with the hardest at 10, these are:

1	Talc	6	Feldspar
2	Gypsum	7	Quartz
3	Calcite	8	Topaz
4	Fluorspar	9	Corundum
5	Apatite	10	Diamond

Hardness pencils are manufactured containing a selection of these materials. The test is based on the assumption that a gemstone of a certain hardness number can only be scratched by a material of a higher number. In practice, the scratch is made starting with the lowest number pencil and working up until one is reached which just scratches the surface of the gem. The hardness of the gem will then be one number less than that of the material in the tip of the hardness pencil. Gemstone hardness values are listed in the table of constants in Appendix 2.

Is there a less risky way of checking a gem's hardness?

With unmounted stones a 'reverse' hardness test is much safer. This uses a series of flat polished hardness plates, which can be made up from relatively cheap materials such as quartz (having a hardness of 7), synthetic spinel (8) and synthetic corundum (9). The girdle or circumference of the gem (*not* its facet edges) can then be used to produce a scratch on the surface of the test plates, starting with corundum and working downwards in hardness. When a scratch is produced, the hardness of the gem will be the next number above that of the scratch plate material.

As previously indicated, a scratch test is not often used when identifying a gemstone, as without due care it can be a destructive test, and there are usually other more specific tests which can be made.

Can a diamond be identified by its ability to scratch glass?

Diamond will certainly scratch glass with ease, but as glass is relatively soft (5 to 6) it can also be scratched by several of the diamond simulants, such as YAG, synthetic spinel and zirconia. A more positive test is to check the stone's ability to produce a scratch on the polished face of a test plate made from synthetic corundum. Because diamond is the only gem harder than corundum, no other stone is capable of marking the plate.

Does a gem's hardness affect the method by which it is polished?

From the gem polisher's or lapidary's point of view, the hardness of a gem dictates the type of surface he uses on his *lap* or polishing wheel, the grade of abrasive powder he uses to cut and polish the stone, and the speed at which he rotates the lap.

Although it may be quicker to shape or preform a soft gemstone, it is usually easier to achieve a good high polish on the harder gemstones.

Varying grades and types of abrasive powder are used first to grind the facet faces and then to polish them. With diamond polishing, the facets are ground and polished using diamond powder as there is no other material hard enough to polish diamond.

As they both have the same hardness, how can diamond dust polish a diamond?

This is only possible because of a property called *directional hardness*, which is possessed by several gems, and especially by diamond. Directional hardness is really a crystalline property.

Diamond, for instance, has a hardness of 10 only in certain directions. In other directions its hardness is significantly lower. As the minute particles of diamond dust used to both polish and saw a diamond are randomly positioned, some of them will be in the direction of maximum hardness, and provided that the polisher avoids the planes of maximum hardness in the diamond he is polishing, all will be well. The same reasoning applies when a diamond is sawn in two using a diamond-dust impregnated saw wheel.

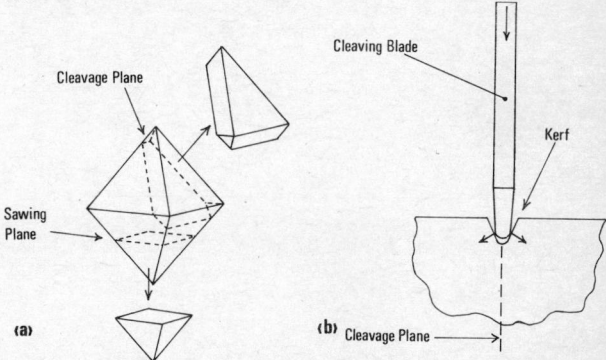

Fig. 6. *(a) The sawing and cleavage planes in an octahedral diamond. (b) The wedge effect of the diamond cleaving blade*

As diamond, in common with other crystalline gems, has a *grain*, this also has to be taken into account. Rather like a piece of wood, diamond is most easily cut across the grain, and with a typical eight-sided diamond crystal this is in a direct parallel to the 'girdle' formed by the junction of the two pyramid-shaped halves (*Fig. 6a*).

Is directional hardness the property which allows a gemstone such as diamond to be divided in two?

No, there is another crystalline property called *cleavage*, which is mainly used when dividing up large irregularly shaped diamonds.

Cleavage in a gemstone is a plane or direction of weak molecular bonding. If we again take a piece of wood as an example, this, rather like a gemstone, can be cleaved or split along the direction of its grain.

Not all gemstones possess the property of cleavage, and among those which do, topaz and diamond are examples which are said to have *perfect* cleavage. When a diamond is cleaved, the direction of its 'grain' is first carefully identified, and then a groove or *kerf* is scratched parallel with the cleavage plane. The radiused tip of the cleaving blade is then placed in this groove so that it acts as a wedge to drive the two sections of the diamond apart. The blade is given a sharp tap, and if the cleaver has correctly identified the cleavage plane, the diamond parts cleanly in two (*Fig. 6b*).

What happens if an attempt is made to cleave a gemstone in the wrong direction?

This may cause the gemstone to break or *fracture*. The way in which a gemstone fractures, perhaps as the result of an accidental blow, can also be characteristic of the gem material. Because of this, small edge fractures in a faceted gemstone can sometimes be useful in helping to identify the stone.

For example, a *conchoidal* or shell-like fracture is associated with quartz, the garnets, and especially glass. A *splintery* fracture is typical of the jade minerals and of ivory. A *broken* or *uneven* fracture, seen in most rocks, is a characteristic of amber. A *smooth* or featureless fracture, which, while reasonably flat, cannot be mistaken for a cleavage plane, can often be seen in a damaged diamond crystal.

Does the composition of a gem affect any other property?

The *density* or *specific gravity* of a gemstone is dependent upon the atomic weights of the various elements in the stone's chemical formula, as well as on the compactness of the structure formed by these elements.

Is there a difference between a gemstone's density and its specific gravity?

Numerically, both of these are the same. The *density* of a gemstone is defined as its mass per unit volume, and is given in terms of kilograms per cubic metre (e.g. the density of diamond = 3520 kg/m^3). The *specific gravity* of a gemstone, however, is the ratio between the mass of the stone and the mass of an identical volume of pure water at 4°C (e.g. the specific gravity of diamond = 3.52). Of these two, specific gravity is the constant used most frequently in gemmology. Gemstone specific gravities are listed in the table in Appendix 2.

How is the density of a gemstone measured in practice?

There are two main methods. One of these is called *hydrostatic weighing*, and consists of weighing the gem on a precision

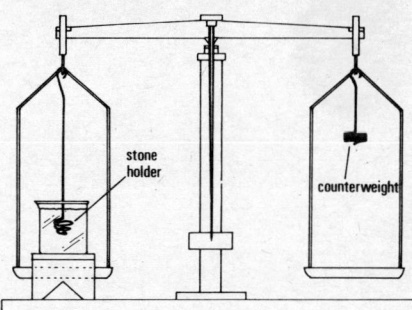

Fig. 7. *Accessories required for hydrostatic weighing are a wire stone holder, a glass beaker, a beaker support and a counterweight (cut to balance exactly the weight of the stone holder when it is immersed in water). For the 'in air' weighing, the gemstone is placed in the left-hand side pan and weighed in the conventional manner, with the stone holder and counterweight removed*

balance, first in air and then when it is completely immersed in water (*Fig. 7*). The gem's specific gravity (or S.G. for short) can then be calculated by subtracting the 'in water' weighing from the 'in air' weighing (to obtain the apparent loss in weight due to the displacement of water), and then dividing this figure into the 'in air' weight. For maximum accuracy, the water should be at 4°C (or an allowance made for departures from this figure) as this is the temperature at which water is at its most dense.

The second method of determining a gemstone's S.G. is to immerse it, in turn, in a series of standard 'heavy' liquids of various specific gravities. This will normally indicate that the gemstone's S.G. is greater than that of the liquid in which it sinks, and less than that of the liquid in which it floats. On the rare occasions when the gemstone floats slowly up and down in one of the liquids it will have exactly the same S.G. as the test liquid. As quartz is a fairly common gemstone, with a specific gravity of 2.65, one of the test liquids is usually made up to this value.

What type of liquids are used for this test?

Many 'heavy' liquids have been experimented with in the past, but the two in general use today are bromoform, which has an S.G. of 2.89, and methylene iodide, with an S.G. of 3.32. A third liquid is also used very occasionally. This is Clerici's solution (S.G. = 4.15), and as it is an unpleasant and corrosive mixture, it must be handled with care. For this reason it is not in general everyday use.

Another liquid, monobromonaphthalene (with an S.G. of 1.49) is used to dilute bromoform to 2.65 (the S.G. for quartz), and to dilute methylene iodide to 3.05 (the S.G. for tourmaline). When Clerici's solution is used, this can be diluted with water to, for example, 3.52, the S.G. for diamond.

The method of dilution is to insert a piece of indicator material (e.g. quartz or tourmaline) in the heavy liquid, and to add the dilutant slowly (while stirring) until the indicator just floats between the surface of the liquid and the bottom of the container.

Is there a physical size limit to the measurement of S.G. by hydrostatic weighing?

Yes, with stones which only displace a small amount of water, the difference between the weight 'in air' and 'in water' is very small and is difficult to measure accurately. The practical lower limit, for accurate results, is about 2 carats in size. There is also a practical upper limit to the size of the sample. The S.G. of a sizeable carving, for instance, cannot easily be measured using a precision balance. In this case a reasonable approximation to the object's S.G. can be made by means of a spring balance and a large container of water. Although the weighing accuracy is poor with the spring balance, the size of the object and the correspondingly large difference between the 'in air' and 'in water' weighing produces reasonable results.

4
Gem crystals

Uncut gem minerals often have very symmetrical shapes; what causes this?

In Chapter 1 we described how gem minerals slowly crystallised out of the molten rocks, or from chemically-rich aqueous solutions, as the primeval earth began to cool. This ability of gem minerals (and some man-made gems) to form crystals is the reason why they often occur, or crystallise, in symmetrical shapes such as prisms and cubes.

What exactly is a crystal?

The word 'crystal' is derived from the Greek *krystallos* meaning ice or frost, and in the past has been used to label anything which was colourless and transparent, like ice; hence the name 'rock crystal' for the colourless variety of quartz.

Although the crystals we are concerned with in gemmology are either mineral or man-made substances, there are also crystals which are composed of materials such as naphthalene or sugar which have an organic origin.

Gem crystals can form in two main ways. The first of these is where the gem's chemical constituents are in a molten state and exist within a body of molten magma or rock. As this magma cools, a point is reached where the gem mineral begins to solidify as a crystal or a series of crystals. In the second way, the gem constituents may be dissolved in a solution of water. This occurs because at high pressures the boiling point of water is sufficiently high to allow materials such as quartz to dissolve in the resulting superheated water (this forms the basis of the *hydrothermal* technique for growing synthetic quartz crystals).

However, there is a limit to the amount of material that can be dissolved in water, and this limit drops with falling temperature. As the chemically-rich gem liquid cools, therefore, a point is eventually reached where it becomes *supersaturated*, which means that it contains more material than it can hold. At this point crystals of the dissolved gem material start to grow, and continue growing until the liquid is no longer in a supersaturated state.

If the temperature falls fast, a multitude of very small crystals will be formed. If the temperature falls very gradually, the result will be fewer, but larger crystals.

What is it that produces symmetry in a crystal?

The atoms and molecules which make up a crystal are arranged in a regular three-dimensional structure or lattice. This resulting symmetry shows itself in the outward shape or *habit* of the crystal. In a non-crystalline material, there is no such regular internal arrangement, and because of this such a substance cannot have a naturally-occurring external shape. For this reason, non-crystalline materials are described as being *amorphous* (i.e. shapeless). Examples of amorphous gems can be seen in organic materials such as amber, jet and ivory.

Are all organic gems amorphous?

No; coral, for instance, consists of minute crystals of calcite, and another crystalline form of calcite, called *aragonite*, is contained in the growth layers of both natural and cultured pearls.

What is the reason for the differences in crystal shapes?

Depending on their chemical composition, all crystalline materials belong to one of seven *crystal systems*. These systems vary from the very symmetrical *cubic* system, to the less regular *triclinic* system. Another factor which results in variations in shape, or *habit*, between minerals, even when they belong to the same crystal system, is the way in which their chemical composition modifies the basic crystal profile. These variations can be produced by the development of extra terminating or end facets, or by the intergrowth of multiple crystals.

How do the seven crystal systems differ from one another?

The main difference, as already indicated, is one of symmetry. The basic shape and symmetry of the seven crystal systems is defined by using imaginary lines of reference called *axes*, which pass through the centres of the crystal faces to meet at a point

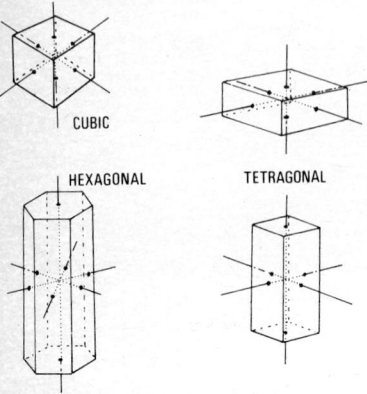

Fig. 8. *The axes and basic shapes of the cubic, tetragonal and hexagonal crystal systems*

30

inside the crystal called the *origin*. In *crystallography*, or the science of crystal structures, each of the basic crystal system shapes is described in terms of the number and length of these axes, and their angular relationships to one another.

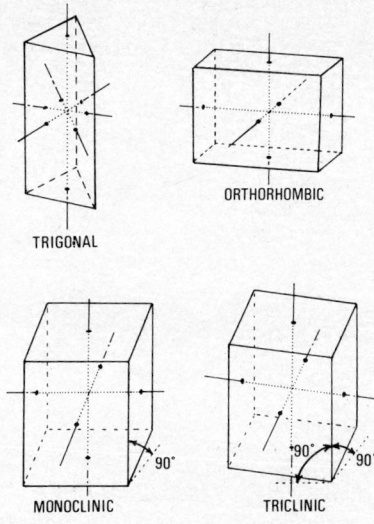

TRIGONAL

ORTHORHOMBIC

MONOCLINIC

TRICLINIC

Fig. 9. *The axes and basic shapes of the trigonal, orthorhombic, monoclinic and triclinic crystal systems*

The best way to illustrate the differences between the seven systems is by means of sketches (*Figs. 8* and *9*). The numbers and relationships of the axes in each system are as follows:

Cubic. Three axes, all of equal length and intersecting one another at right-angles. Examples: diamond, fluorspar, garnet, pyrite, spinel.

Tetragonal. Two equal length axes at right-angles to each other, and a third axis which is either shorter or longer than the other two, and at right-angles to them. Examples: rutile, scapo-lite, zircon.

Hexagonal. Four axes, the first three being of equal length and intersecting each other at 60° in the same plane. The fourth axis is at right-angles to the others and usually longer. Examples: apatite, beryl (emerald, aquamarine).

Trigonal. This also has four axes which are arranged in the same manner as in the hexagonal system. The overall symmetry of the trigonal system is, however, lower than that of the hexagonal system. Examples: corundum (ruby, sapphire), quartz, rhodochrosite, tourmaline.

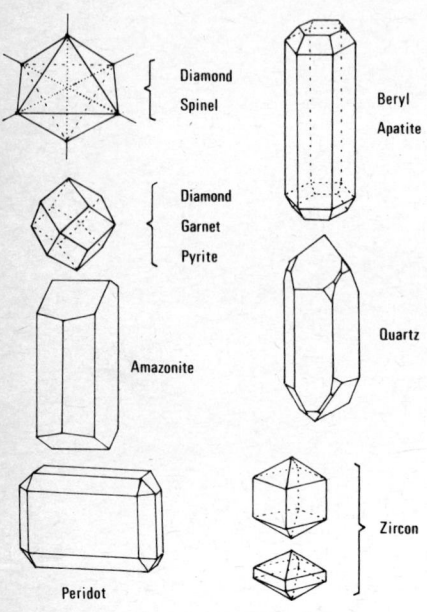

Fig. 10. *Examples of commonly occurring crystalline shapes*

Orthorhombic. Three axes, all at right-angles to one another, but (unlike the cubic system) all of different lengths. Examples: chrysoberyl, peridot, topaz.

Monoclinic. Three axes, all of different lengths. Two axes meet each other at angles other than 90°. The third axis is at right-angles to the other two. Examples: feldspar (moonstone), diopside, malachite, spodumene, titanite (sphene).

Triclinic. Three axes, all of different lengths and all inclined to one another at angles other than 90°. Examples: feldspar (amazonite, labradorite, sunstone), rhodonite.

The habits of some of the more common of these gem crystals are shown in the sketches in *Fig. 10.*

Apart from appearance, are there other differences between crystals in the seven systems?

There are two basic optical differences between gems in the seven crystal systems which will be more fully explained in Chapter 5 under 'Optical properties of gemstones'. One of these differences exists between gems in the cubic crystal system (which are all *singly-refracting*), and gems in the remaining six systems (which are all *doubly-refracting*). The other difference is that gems in the tetragonal, hexagonal and trigonal systems all possess a single *optical axis*, while gems in the orthorhombic, monoclinic and triclinic systems possess *two* optical axes.

Can a knowledge of crystallography help in identifying gems?

At its simplest level, crystallography can be used as a guide to the optical properties and characteristics present in gemstones. With rough mineral specimens, the crystal habit of a particular species or variety can often be distinctive enough to allow positive identification, and even where this is not possible it will usually provide a good indication of the gem's crystal system.

What is meant by a crypto-crystalline gem?

A few crystalline gemstones, including chalcedony (agate, chrysoprase, onyx), coral, jade (jadeite, nephrite) and turquoise, are composed not of a single crystal, but of a multitude of tiny crystals or crystalline fibres. This micro-crystalline structure usually results in an opaque or translucent gem material, and also has a significant effect on the gem's optical properties. Crypto-crystalline gems, because of their internal structure, have slightly porous surfaces, and this characteristic is sometimes made use of by staining the stones to improve their colour.

The internal structure of crypto-crystalline gems also affects their outward form, which is always *massive* (this is a term used to describe minerals having no definite external crystal habit).

As rose quartz samples are 'massive', does this mean that they are crypto-crystalline?

No, rose quartz is a truly *macro-crystalline* gem (as opposed to a micro- or crypto-crystalline gem). However, the manganese impurity which causes the gem's colour also prevents the stone from forming an outward crystal shape (except in rare specimens). There are several other gems which are not crypto-crystalline materials, but which often occur in massive form (e.g. apatite, pyrite, rhodochrosite, rhodonite, rutile, scapolite).

5
Optical properties of gemstones

Apart from hardness, cleavage and specific gravity, what other properties are possessed by a gemstone?

Perhaps the most important gemstone properties, both from an aesthetic and an identification point of view, are those associated with their optical behaviour, and include refractive index, double refraction, pleochroism, dispersion, lustre and sheen.

What is meant by refractive index?

When light rays travelling through air enter an optically denser medium, such as a transparent gemstone, they are bent or *refracted* from their original path (*Fig. 11*). The greater the amount of bending or refraction, the greater the *refractive index* of the stone. The refractive index of a material is expressed theoretically as the relationship between the angles of the *incident* ray and the *refracted* ray. These angles are measured between each ray and an imaginary line called the *normal*, which is drawn at right-angles to the surface of the material. *Snell's law of refraction* defines a material's refractive index (or R.I. for short) as follows:

$$\text{R.I.} = \frac{\text{Sine of incident ray angle}}{\text{Sine of refracted ray angle}}$$

Snell's law also states that the incident ray, the refracted ray and the 'normal' (at the point of incidence) all lie in the same plane, and that the R.I. of a material is dependent on the surrounding medium (normally air) and on the wavelength or colour of the light (a point of some importance in gemmology).

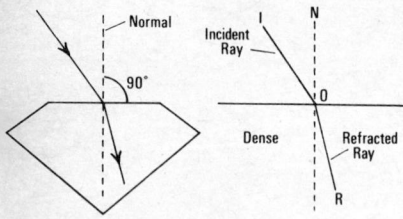

Fig. 11. Light rays are refracted towards the 'normal' as they enter an optically denser medium (such as a gemstone) and are refracted away from the normal when they pass into a rarer medium (such as air)

Because the measurement of the R.I. of a material is affected by the wavelength or colour of the illumination, the convention adopted in gemmology is to quote gemstone R.I.s in terms of yellow sodium light (having a precise wavelength of 589.3 nm). Sodium light is chosen as a reference because it is *monochromatic* (i.e. it is a pure colour with all its energy concentrated at one wavelength) and is relatively easy to produce.

The R.I. of a gemstone and the effects of the refraction of light are of some importance in gemmology, and as an aid to understanding some of these effects it should be remembered that a light ray entering a gemstone from air (at angles other than perpendicular) is refracted *towards* the normal, and a ray leaving the gemstone and passing into air is refracted *away* from the normal. (R.I. values of gemstones are included in Appendix 2.)

Why is the R.I. of a gemstone so important in gemmology?

The R.I. of a gem is, in general, a very constant and characteristic figure for each species, and as it can be measured with high accuracy it is of great help in the identification of gemstones.

How is a gemstone's R.I. measured?

There are several methods, the most precise of which involves the use of an instrument called a *refractometer*. This provides a precise reading of a gemstone's R.I. by using the optical phenomenon known as the *critical angle of total reflection*.

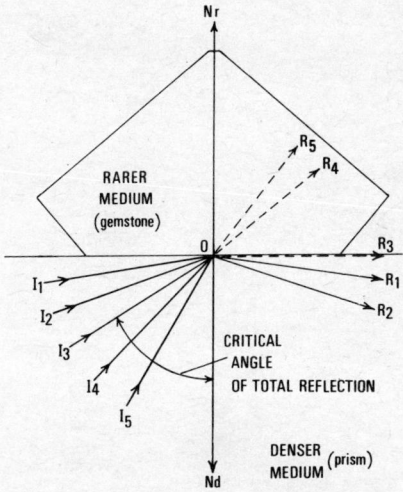

Fig. 12. *Incident rays (I_1, I_2) at angles greater than the critical angle are reflected (R_1, R_2), while rays equal to or less than the critical angle (I_3, I_4, I_5) are refracted (R_3, R_4, R_5)*

If the polished surface of a gemstone is placed in contact with the surface of a transparent material having a higher R.I. (e.g. optically dense lead glass), rays passing through this latter material will be reflected back from the surface of the gemstone provided that the angle between the rays and the normal is greater than the *critical angle* (I_1, I_2 and R_1, R_2 in *Fig. 12*). Rays equal to or less than this critical angle will either be refracted along the surface of the gemstone (I_3, R_3) or refracted into the gemstone (I_4, R_4 and I_5, R_5).

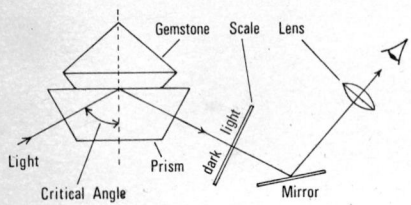

Fig. 13. *Principal components in a refractometer, which uses the phenomenon of critical angle to measure the refractive indices of gemstones*

The critical angle between the gemstone and the denser material is entirely dependent on the respective R.I.s of the two materials. If the optically dense medium is, in fact, a prism in a refractometer (*Fig. 13*), then the R.I. of the gemstone can be directly related to the position of a shadow line (created by the reflected and refracted light rays) superimposed on a calibrated scale.

Provided that the gemstone's R.I. is within the instrument's measuring range, the only other requirement to the production of a visible shadow edge reading is a good optical contact between the surface of the gemstone and that of the refractometer prism. This is ensured by the use of a drop of *contact liquid*, which effectively excludes any air from the junction between the gemstone and the prism. The R.I. of this coupling fluid must be at least as high as the highest R.I. reading on the refractometer, so as to avoid the introduction of a further shadow edge on the operational part of the refractometer scale, and to maintain its full measuring range.

What is the measuring range of a refractometer?

On standard instruments, using optically dense lead glass, the range is normally 1.34–1.80. The standard contact fluid, blended to make full use of this range, has an R.I. of 1.81, and consists of a saturated solution of sulphur in methylene iodide.

To assist in the identification of gemstones having higher refractive indices than 1.80, several extended-range refracto- meters have been developed with prisms having much higher R.I. values. These have included versions using blende, diamond and strontium titanate measuring prisms. The blende and diamond refractometers (made by the Rayner Optical Company) had ranges of 1.59–2.03, the top end being limited by the contact liquid (an unpleasant concoction of phosphorus and sulphur in methylene iodide, with an R.I. of 2.05).

The more recent strontium titanate version (made by Krüss) has a range of 1.75–2.21, the higher top limit being achieved through the use of a contact paste which only becomes liquid when heated to 40°C. To maintain the paste in its liquid form, the instrument's strontium titanate prism is also heated to 40°C by means of an electrical element.

What kind of light source is used with a refractometer?

Ideally, a sodium light source should be used for best results. The reason for this is not simply because gemstone R.I. values are quoted in terms of yellow sodium light, but because the shadow edge on the scale of the refractometer is more distinct when using a monochromatic light source (if a white light source is used, the shadow edge is blurred into a spectrum of colour due to differences in certain optical characteristics between the gemstone under test and the measuring prism).

Unfortunately, a sodium light source is expensive, and this is often replaced with a strong yellow-filtered white light source, or even by yellow light-emitting diodes (L.E.D.s), both of which can be chosen to provide an emission peak close to the sodium wavelength of 589.3 nm. Another alternative is to use a strong source of white light and to place a deep yellow filter over the refractometer eyepiece.

What is meant by a doubly-refracting gem?

Double refraction (or D.R. for short) occurs in gems belonging to the tetragonal, hexagonal, trigonal, orthorhombic, monoclinic and triclinic crystal systems. Gems in these systems have *two* refractive indices (and are sometimes described as being *anisotropic* or *birefringent*), while gems which are amorphous, or which belong to the cubic crystal system, have only *one* refractive index and are called *isotropic*.

What happens to light rays entering a doubly-refracting gem?

The light entering a doubly-refracting gem is split into two separate rays which are polarised at right-angles to each other. Each set of rays is diffracted by a different amount as it enters and leaves the gem.

When checked on a refractometer, a doubly-refracting gem will produce *two* shadow edges on the scale. To measure the amount of double refraction, the gem is rotated on the refractometer measuring prism until the two shadow edges are farthest apart (for orthorhombic, monoclinic and triclinic gems the maximum and minimum shadow edge readings will not necessarily occur together as the stone is rotated). The D.R. value for the gem is then obtained by subtracting the lowest reading from the highest one. In the same way that the R.I. of a gemstone is characteristic of the gem species, its D.R. often provides a valuable identifying feature.

What is polarised light?

Ordinary unpolarised light contains rays which are vibrating in *all* directions at right-angles to their line of travel (like the spokes of a bicycle wheel). With polarised light, the rays only vibrate in *one* direction or plane at right-angles to the line of travel.

Light reflected off the surface of the sea contains a large proportion of *horizontally* polarised rays. The dazzle of reflected light from horizontal surfaces is reduced in some sunglasses by fitting them with *vertically* polarised lenses.

What other methods are there for measuring the R.I.?

If a microscope with a calibrated focus control is available, the R.I. of a gem can be measured by what is called the 'direct' method. This consists of securing the gem on the stage of the microscope with its main (table) facet uppermost and the tip of its pavilion in contact with the stage. The microscope is then focused on the surface of the table facet, and then down through the stone to the tip of its pavilion to produce two focus readings which represent the *apparent depth* of the gem. The *real* depth of the stone can then be found by removing the stone and focusing on to the surface of the stage. The R.I. of the gem is arrived at by dividing the apparent depth into the real depth. This method, however, only produces an approximate figure, and cannot be used to measure double refraction. Despite this, it can be of value when it is necessary to check a stone whose R.I. is above the range of the standard recfractometer.

Another method of approximating the R.I. of a gemstone, is to immerse it, in turn, in a series of liquids, each having a different known R.I. The method depends on the fact that when a material is immersed in a liquid having a similar R.I., reflections from the surface of the material are much reduced, and its outline becomes indistinct (this happens, for example, when an ice cube is immersed in water). Suitable liquids for this test, and their appropriate refractive indices, are as follows:

Water	1.33	Iodobenzene	1.62
Alcohol	1.36	Monobromonaphthalene	1.66
Petrol	1.45	Iodonaphthalene	1.70
Benzene	1.50	Methylene iodide	1.74
Clove oil	1.54	Refractometer contact liquid	1.81
Bromoform	1.59		

Is it possible to detect the presence of D.R. in a gemstone without using a refractometer?

If a gemstone is inspected through its top crown facets using a hand lens, it is possible with stones which possess a large D.R. to see a distinct double image of the rear facet junctions. This is particularly noticeable with the majority of zircons, whose D.R. is 0.058, and with practice it can also be seen in peridot (0.038), sinhalite (0.038) and tourmaline (0.018).

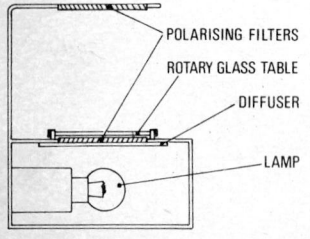

POLARISING FILTERS

ROTARY GLASS TABLE

DIFFUSER

LAMP

Fig. 14. *Construction of a polari-scope which is used to test for single refraction, double refraction and for a crypto-crystalline response*

D.R. can also be detected, but not measured, by using a simple instrument called a *polariscope*. This consists of a light source and two pieces of polarising filter (*Fig. 14*). The gemstone under test is placed on the lower filter (which is protected by a piece of glass), and the top filter is set in the 'crossed' position, where it rejects or 'extinguishes' the polarised light from the bottom filter.

If the gem is rotated through 360°, and is a doubly-refracting stone, the light passing through the stone (as viewed through the top filter) will appear to go from bright to dark four times for each complete rotation (i.e. at 90° intervals). If the stone remains mainly dark when rotated, it is either an amorphous material or belongs to the cubic crystal system.

As doubly-refracting gems have one or two directions along which they appear to be singly-refracting, it is important that tests on the polariscope are carried out with the stone in at least two different positions.

Some singly-refracting gems, such as diamond, glass and synthetic spinel, contain internal stresses and strains, and often show some signs of D.R. on the polariscope (this is known as *anomalous* double refraction). However, when this happens it is never as clearly defined as the more positive light and dark effect seen with a doubly-refracting stone.

Apart from the detection of D.R., the polariscope can also be usefully employed to detect paste or glass gems by means of their very distinctive internal stresses, which appear as a strong cross-pattern of dark lines. Other gems whose optical character can be identified on the polariscope are the crypto-crystalline stones such as chalcedony (agate, onyx, chrysoprase, etc), jadeite and nephrite. As these gemstones are composed of a multitude of randomly positioned crystals or crystalline fibres, they always transmit light no matter which way they are turned (with opaque specimens, this test can be made by watching the small amount of light leaking through the thinner edges of the stone).

What is pleochroism?

The two polarised rays travelling through a *coloured doubly-refracting* gem may each have different sections of their spectrum absorbed by the stone. When this happens it is called *differential selective absorption*, and the two rays emerge from the stone differing either in colour, or in depth of colour. The effect is called *pleochroism*. Stones which produce two colours or shades are *dichroic*, and those which produce three are *trichroic*.

How can pleochroism be detected?

With strongly pleochroic stones, such as andalusite and iolite, the various colours can be seen with the naked eye by simply rotating

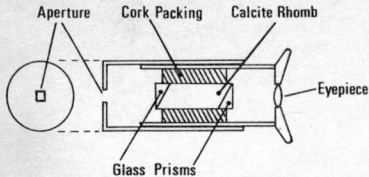

Fig. 15. *Pleochroism in a doubly-refracting coloured gem is detected by a dichroscope which separates the two polarised rays*

Table 3. Colours of strongly pleochroic gems

Gemstone	Pleochroic colours
Alexandrite	Daylight: *green*, yellowish, pink Tungsten light: *red*, yellowish-red, green
Andalusite	*Green*, yellow, red
Apatite	*Blue*, colourless
Hiddenite	*Green*, yellowish-green, bluish-green
Iolite	*Pale blue*, dark blue, pale yellow
Kornerupine	*Green*, yellow, brown
Kunzite	*Pink*, purple, colourless
Ruby	*Deep red*, yellowish-pink
Sapphire	*Blue*, greenish-blue
Sinhalite	*Green*, yellow, brown
Tourmaline	Two shades of body colour
Zoisite	*Blue*, purple, brown

the stone. With less obvious examples, the effect is best seen with the aid of a dichroscope (*Fig. 15*). This instrument either contains a piece of iceland spar (optically pure calcite), or a flat polarising filter, and this enables the two polarised rays to be separated for side-by-side comparison in the eyepiece.

When the dichroscope is used to help identify a gem, the stone must be inspected in several different directions. This requirement is necessary because there are certain directions in which a doubly-refracting stone will not show pleochroism, even if it exists. *Table 3* lists the colours of strongly pleochroic gems.

Is pleochroism an attractive feature in a gem?

With some gems, such as andalusite, pleochroism is attractive, and the rough crystal will be carefully polished so as to make all the colours visible through the top of the stone. However, with other gems (e.g. ruby and sapphire) one of the dichroic colours is less attractive than the other, and the gem will be cut so that this colour is less visible.

What is dispersion in a gem?

In diamond, the property of dispersion is responsible for the multi-coloured flashes of 'fire' seen when the polished gem is

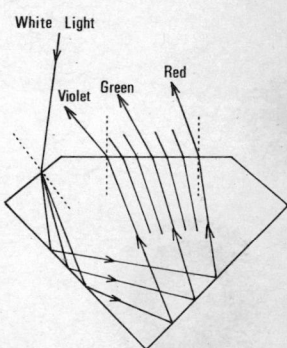

Fig. 16. Coloured 'fire' in a gem is produced by the dispersion of white light into its spectral components, and is enhanced by the total internal reflection of the rays within the gem

moved under a multi-point light source. Dispersion in gemstones varies from being strong and noticeable in diamond and zircon, to weak and difficult to detect in colourless sapphire and topaz. Noticeable dispersion of light into its spectral colours occurs when the medium through which the light is passing has an R.I. which is considerably higher at the blue end of the spectrum than it is at the red end. This causes the components in the spectrum to be refracted by different amounts, and to emerge as individual colours (*Fig. 16*).

The dispersion of a gemstone is, in fact, measured as the difference in its R.I. at two reference wavelengths in the red and blue ends of the spectrum (known as the B and G Fraunhofer wavelengths at 686.7 nm and 430.8 nm respectively).

What is the difference between a gem's lustre and its sheen?

The lustre of a gem is entirely due to the degree by which light is reflected off the *surface* of the gem. Sheen is the result of light being reflected back from *beneath* the surface of the gem.

Lustre can be described in relative terms such as *metallic* for materials having the highest reflectivity, *adamantine* (for diamond), *vitreous* (for the majority of gems), *waxy* and *greasy* (jadeite and soapstone, respectively).

There are several characteristic types of sheen including *chatoyancy* (cat's eye effect), *asterism* (star effect) and *iridescence* (the 'play' of colour seen in opal). All of these are caused by light-reflecting features beneath the surface of the gem.

Chatoyancy and asterism are both caused by parallel sets of needles, fibres or channels within the stone. In tiger's eye and cat's eye stones there is one set of parallel inclusions, but in star sapphires and rubies there are three sets intersecting each other at 60°.

Iridescence, or 'play' of colour, is caused by extremely small regular structures beneath the surface of the gemstone which 'interfere' with the reflected light, reinforcing some colours and cancelling others (in opal this is due to millions of microscopic cristobalite spheres).

6
Luminescence and electrical properties

What is meant by luminescence?

Although solid materials are able to radiate visible light when their temperature is raised to a point where they become 'red hot' or 'white hot', there are some substances which are capable of radiating light at very much lower temperatures. This 'cold' light is known as *luminescence*.

What causes a substance to luminesce?

Luminescence is caused by the 'excitation' of atoms within the substance, and this condition can be brought about by the application of relatively low levels of energy in one form or another. This energy enables the electrons orbiting the nucleus of the atom to jump into higher level but less stable orbits. When the electrons finally fall back into their original orbits, they give up their surplus energy in the form of a visible radiation or luminescence.

What kind of energy produces luminescence?

Luminescing materials can be divided into various categories, each one requiring energy in a particular form before it can produce its characteristic 'cold' radiation.

Some materials luminesce when they are exposed to energy in the form of electromagnetic radiation (i.e. visible light, ultra-violet light or X-rays). This type of response is called *photoluminescence*. Other substances glow when they are rubbed or scratched, and in this case the effect is known as *triboluminescence*. Still other materials, such as the phosphors on the screen of a television tube, luminesce when bombarded with energy in the form of electrons, and this type of cold radiation is called *cathodoluminescence*.

There are several other types of luminescence brought about, for instance, by the application of energy in the form of an electric current (electroluminescence) or by means of chemical action (as with phosphorus and with fire flies). Of all these various types, the most useful one for the identification of gemstones is photoluminescence. This is mainly because the wavelength of the emitted radiation is always longer than that of the applied excitation, and this results in the production of visible luminescence from sources of invisible radiation such as U.-V. light and

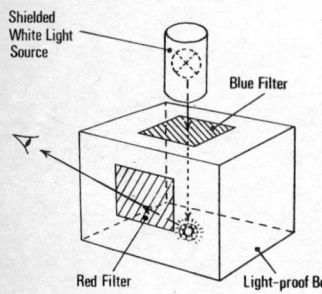

Fig. 17. *A test unit, using the 'crossed filter' technique, for identifying red fluorescence in gems illuminated by blue light*

X-rays. Even blue light can stimulate some gemstones into luminescing in the longer wavelength red end of the spectrum. This latter phenomenon can be made visible by the use of 'crossed filters', which is perhaps the simplest method of detecting luminescence in a gemstone.

All that is required is a strong source of blue-filtered light and a red filter (*Fig. 17*). The blue light can be produced either by means of a flask filled with copper sulphate solution (which has the dual advantage of acting as a heat filter and a condensing lens), or by means of a glass or a gelatine-type filter (the latter being protected from the heat of the lamp by placing it behind a piece of glass).

If only the blue-filtered light is allowed to illuminate the gemstone specimen, and the stone is seen to glow red when viewed through the red filter, then this is proof that it is converting the energy in the blue light into a longer wavelength red luminescence.

What is the difference between luminescence, fluorescence and phosphorescence?

Luminescence is a term which describes all types of 'cold' light radiation. Depending on the characteristic of the emitted light, this can then be classified as *fluorescence* or *phosphorescence*.

The orbital movements of the electrons in a luminescing material occur in a random fashion. If there is virtually no delay between these electrons acquiring energy and then releasing it, the radiation of cold light will cease immediately the excitation is removed, and the effect is described as a *fluorescent* one. However, if there is an appreciable delay before the electrons give up their surplus energy, the phenomenon is known as *phosphorescence*, and is visible as an after-glow when the excitation ceases.

With all types of luminescence, the radiated light is either caused by some characteristic property of the substance, or is due to the presence of luminescent impurities called *actuators*.

Why is luminescence useful in gemstone identification?

Many gem materials have distinctive and characteristic intensities and colours of fluorescence and phosphorescence. These luminescent characteristics may vary with the wavelength of the irradiation source (i.e. long-wave U.-V. at 366 nm, short-wave U.-V. at 254 nm, or X-rays at 0.1–1.0 nm), or may only occur at specific wavelengths. *Table 4* lists the fluorescent and phosphorescent effects seen in the principal gem materials.

Table 4. Fluorescent and phosphorescent effects in the principal gems

Gemstone	L.W. U.-V.	S.W. U.-V.	X-rays
Apatite, yellow	Lilac	Lilac/pink	Pinkish-white/yellow
Apatite, blue	Blue	Blue	Pinkish straw (faint)
Danburite	Blue (medium)	Blue	Violet
Diamond (only 10–15% of diamonds luminesce under U.-V.)	Blue,* green, yellow, pink or red	Similar to L.W. but occurrence irregular	Chalky blue (consistent)
Emerald (natural)	Red (some)	Red (some)	Red
Emerald (synthetic)	Red (strong)	Red (strong)	Red
Fluorspar (none in 'Blue John')	Blue/violet (strong)	Blue/violet (weak)	Blue, violet
GGG (gadolinium gallium garnet)	Straw colour (weak)	Peach colour	Lilac
Hydrogrossular garnet ('Transvaal Jade')	–	–	Orange
Kunzite	Orange	–	Orange (strong)
Lapis lazuli	Orange (patchy)	–	–

50

Opal (natural)	White, blue, brown, green (weak),† or no fluorescence		Green (some)
Opal (Gilson)	Random	Dusty green	–
Paste	–	Pale blue or green	Green, blue (some)
Ruby (natural)	Red (strong)	Red (strong)	Red (strong)
Ruby (synthetic)	Red (strong)	Red (strong)	Red (strong, with phosphorescence)
Sapphire (white, natural)	Orange	Orange	Crimson
Sapphire (white, synthetic)	–	Deep blue (weak)	Red (variable)
Sapphire (yellow, natural from Sri Lanka)	Yellow	–	Orange
Sapphire (yellow, synthetic)	–	–	Violet (some)
Sapphire (orange, synthetic)	R● (strong)	Red	Red with phosphorescence
Sapphire (blue, natural)	–	–	Red
Sapphire (blue, synthetic)	–	Greenish-blue	Blue
Scapolite	Yellow	Pink	White, orange, green
Spinel (green, yellow, synthetic)	Green (strong, when coloured by manganese)	–	Red (green spinel), green (yellow spinel)

Table 4 continued

Gemstone	L.W. U.-V.	S.W. U.-V.	X-rays
Spinel (blue, synthetic)	Red	–	Red, blue
Spinel (blue, natural)	–	–	–
Spinel (white, synthetic)	–	Blue/white (strong)	Green or blue
Spinel (red, pink)	Red (strong)	Red (strong)	Red
Strontium titanate	–	–	–
YAG (yttrium aluminium garnet)	Yellow	–	Yellow
Zirconia (cubic zirconium oxide)	–	Greenish yellow (faint) or yellow (distinct)	Whitish

* Diamonds which fluoresce blue have a weak yellow phosphorescence which is diagnostic for diamond.
† All colours often accompanied by a persistent green phosphorescence.

How is ultra-violet light produced?

Ultra-violet light is, of course, an important component in sunlight. For test purposes, however, both long-wave (L.W.) and short-wave (S.W.) U.-V. light is produced by means of a mercury-vapour lamp, as this radiates strongly into the far ultra-violet, and has dominant emission lines or peaks at 366 nm and 254 nm. As mercury-vapour lamps also produce a considerable amount of visible light, special filters are used to suppress all but the required wavelengths.

Ultra-violet test lamps can be purchased as separate S.W. or L.W. units, but because it is often necessary to compare the effects of both types of irradiation on a gemstone, units which combine both L.W. and S.W. outputs are the most convenient types to use.

What about X-ray sources?

Because of their cost and the precautions necessary to prevent harmful exposure to the penetrating high-energy rays, X-radiation sources are usually only found in research laboratories. Unlike U.-V. light, X-rays are produced in a vacuum tube by bombarding a tungsten target or plate with high-speed electrons.

Many gemstones produce highly characteristic luminescent effects under X-ray irradiation (see *Table 4*), and for this reason X-ray units are used to obtain valuable diagnostic information in the larger of the gem testing laboratories.

All diamonds fluoresce under X-rays, and this forms an important method of separating diamonds from gravel or rock in the specialised X-ray sorting equipment used in diamond mines.

Are U.-V. rays harmful?

Overlong exposure to U.-V. radiation can damage the eyes, and for this reason it is advisable to avoid looking directly at a U.-V. lamp when making tests. The colour of some gemstones can also be modified by overlong exposure to U.-V. Blue zircons, for instance, can fade under U.-V. (or even after long periods in strong sunlight!), and the diamond simulant GGG (gadolinium gallium garnet) turns brown if left too long under a S.W. U.-V. lamp. The colour of blue zircon can be restored by heating it in air to a dull red temperature, and GGG loses its brown 'suntan' if left in the dark for several hours.

Is U.-V. light used in any other way for gem identification?

There are two other ways in which U.-V. light can be of help when testing gemstones. The first of these is used to distinguish between natural and synthetic emeralds and rubies. The technique employed is called *immersion contact photography*. It consists of placing the test sample, together with a natural stone (as a reference), table facet down on a piece of photographic paper in a darkened room.

The stones and the paper are placed in the bottom of a shallow dish containing water, and exposed to S.W. U.-V. light for two or three seconds (the correct exposure being determined by trial and error). The photographic paper is then developed, and provided that the exposure time is correct, the reference stone will appear white (i.e. it will have absorbed the U.-V. light). The unknown stone, if it is a synthetic emerald or ruby, will appear black with a white rim round its profile, as both of these stones are more transparent to S.W. U.-V. than their natural counterparts.

The second use of U.-V. is when attempting to detect the curved growth lines in synthetic sapphire. When seen, these lines prove that the stone is a synthetic, but they are often very difficult to detect under normal lighting. If the gem is irradiated with U.-V. light, however, the resulting luminescence often increases the structural contrast of the gemstone and makes the growth lines more visible.

Do gemstones possess any identifying electrical properties?

The majority of gemstones are electrically non-conductive, but a few (e.g. haematite, synthetic rutile and blue diamond) will pass an electrical current if a voltage is applied across them. From an identification point of view, the electrical conductivity of natural blue diamond is the most important, as this enables the gem to be distinguished from a non-conducting artificially coloured diamond.

Electrical conductivity in gemstones can be measured as shown in *Fig. 5*, or (with care) by placing the gem on a metal plate connected to the 'line' side of a 100–240 V a.c. supply and using an electrician's screwdriver-type neon tester. If the screwdriver blade is brought into contact with the gem, and a finger placed on the test surface at the end of the screwdriver handle, the neon will glow if the gem is electrically conductive.

Some gemstones, such as tourmaline and topaz, develop an electric charge across the opposite ends of the crystal when heated. This is known as a *pyroelectric* effect. Another electrical effect which is present in both quartz and tourmaline is that of *piezoelectricity*. This results in an electrical potential being developed across the crystal when it is bent or stressed in certain directions. In the case of quartz, the reverse effect, produced by connecting an alternating voltage across the crystal, results in a mechanical oscillation. This effect is made use of in quartz-controlled oscillators and in piezoelectric audio generators (e.g. buzzers and hi-fi 'tweeters').

Amber is well known for its *triboelectric* property, which enables it to develop a static electric charge when rubbed. Although the ability of a suitably charged piece of amber to attract pieces of tissue paper is often used as a test for this gem material, it must be remembered that several of amber's plastic imitators possess the same property, as they are also good electrical insulators.

Another electrical property, called *photoconductivity*, is exhibited by natural blue diamonds. The electrical resistance of these gems drops when they are exposed to gamma radiation, and this makes them suitable for use as radioactive detectors in environments which require a tough corrosion-resistant material.

7
Gemstone cuts and gem polishing

What determines the shape in which a gemstone is polished?

The shape, or *cut*, of a gemstone is determined by a variety of factors. If the gemstone is colourless, one of the requirements will be to produce a gem having a brilliant overall appearance. This will necessitate a cut which will ensure that as many rays as possible entering the stone will be totally internally reflected and returned back through the top facets (*Fig. 16*). If the gem also has a high dispersion, the cut may be modified to ensure that a certain proportion of the rays enter the top of the stone via angled facets to produce the effect of 'fire'. The correct balance between 'brilliance' and 'fire' for diamond is achieved in the ideal proportions and angles of the brilliant cut (*Fig. 18*), which has a total of 57 facets (plus an extra one known as the 'culet', added to remove the otherwise vulnerable point at the bottom of the pavilion).

For coloured stones, it is often preferable to use a cut which brings out the gem's colour to best effect, and examples of this are seen in the *emerald cut* and the *cross-cut* (*Fig. 19*). Practical considerations, such as the shock-sensitivity of emerald, may also dictate that the corners of a particular cut are bevelled to prevent the stone from being damaged. As the R.I. of zircon is lower than that of diamond, the 'zircon cut' (based on the brilliant cut) has an extra eight pavilion facets to prevent leakage of light through the rear of the stone. Semi-translucent and opaque stones, and those with special sheen effects (e.g. cat's eye and star stones), are usually cut in the domed *cabochon* shape.

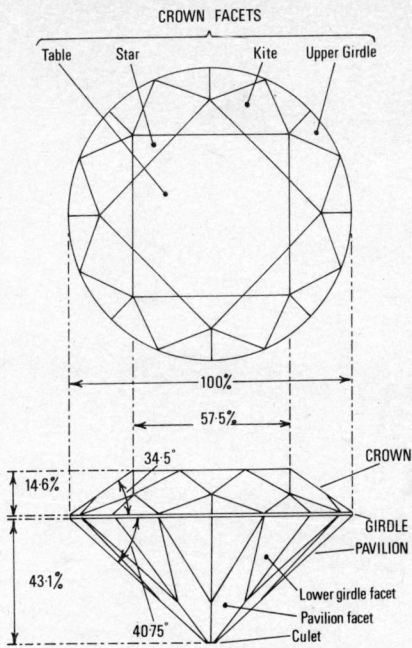

CROWN FACETS

Table Star Kite Upper Girdle

100%

57·5%

34·5°

14·6%

CROWN

GIRDLE

PAVILION

43·1%

Lower girdle facet

Pavilion facet

40·75°

Culet

Fig. 18. The ideal angles and proportions of a brilliant-cut diamond. There are, in fact, several 'ideal' proportions, the one illustrated being the Scan. D.N. standard favoured in Europe. In America, the preferred cut is the Tolkowsky version which has a slightly smaller table (53%) and a deeper crown (16.2%)

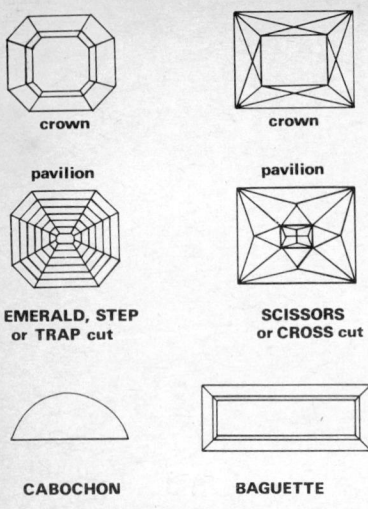

crown

crown

pavilion

pavilion

EMERALD, STEP
or TRAP cut

SCISSORS
or CROSS cut

CABOCHON

BAGUETTE

Fig. 19. *Coloured stone cutting styles
include the emerald cut, the cross-cut
and the domed cabochon (the latter used
mainly for opaque gems, and cat's eye
and star stones)*

Why are some gems cut with a very deep pavilion?

This is done in order to produce a brilliant appearance with gem
materials (such as sapphire and zircon) which have a lower R.I.
than, for example, diamond. The lower the R.I. of the gem, the
deeper must its pavilion be cut in order to bend or refract the rays
sufficiently to achieve total internal reflection.

What alternative cuts are used for diamond?

In addition to the round brilliant cut, there are also the *marquise*,
the *oval* and the *pendeloque* or *pear shape* cuts (*Fig. 20*). All of
these have 57 facets just like the round brilliant cut.

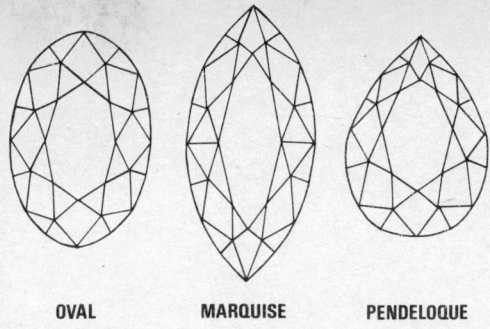

| OVAL | MARQUISE | PENDELOQUE |

Fig. 20. *Variants of the round brilliant-cut diamond all have 33 crown facets and 24 pavilion facets*

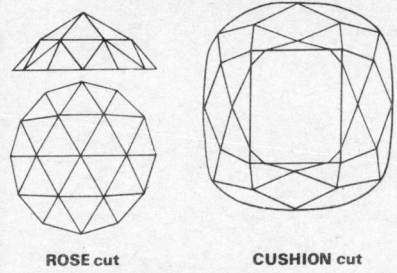

ROSE cut   **CUSHION** cut

Fig. 21. *The rose-cut and cushion-cut styles were in use for diamond long before the modern brilliant cut was involved*

Diamonds are sometimes cut in baguette form, and are also polished as emerald-cut stones. Diamond cutting styles often seen in antique jewellery are the *rose cut* and the *cushion cut* (*Fig. 21*).

What determines the choice of cut with modern diamonds?

As diamond is a very expensive material, the polisher will take great care to achieve the maximum possible yield of polished stones from the rough crystal. If the rough diamond is a symmetrical octahedral crystal, his best yield will be two round brilliant-cut stones (one of these being larger than the other). If, however, the diamond crystal has a distorted shape, the best yield may be achieved if it is cut as an oval, a pear-shaped or a marquise-cut brilliant. For the same reason, an elongated octahedron is sometimes polished in the emerald-cut shape.

Is a diamond ever polished with more than 57 facets?

Several cutting styles have been designed which contain more facets than the brilliant cut. The aim of these more complicated cuts is to achieve a greater degree of brilliance in the finished stone. Examples are the *jubilee cut* (80 facets), the *king cut* (86 facets), the *magna cut* (102 facets) and the *royal cut* (154 facets). Although a degree of extra brilliance can be achieved with these cuts, this has to be offset against the cost of polishing the extra facets. Because of cost, very small diamonds are sometimes polished with only 17 facets (i.e. a table, eight crown facets and eight pavilions). This style is called a *'single cut'*.

The junction between the top crown facets and the lower pavilion facets of a stone (known as the *girdle*) is usually left in the rough-ground state (occasionally with traces of the original crystal surface to show that there has been no wastage!). To improve the overall brilliance of the diamond, this girdle is sometimes given a finishing polish, or is even faceted.

Is the same polishing technique used for all gemstones?

Although the basic concept of shaping and polishing a stone to enhance its beauty is common to all gemstones, there are big differences between the techniques employed in polishing diamonds and those used for the rest of the gemstones.

The reason for this is that diamond is very much harder than any of the other gemstones, and because of this its polishing industry has developed quite separately and uses equipment which is significantly different from that employed to polish the softer gems.

What type of equipment is used for polishing non-diamond gems?

Depending on the size of the rough gem material, either a saw or a grindstone may be used to fashion the rough gem material into manageable pieces. The *lapidary*, or stone polisher, will then grind the stone into its basic profile on a rotary disc, or *lap*, which is coated or impregnated with an abrasive powder such as carborundum or emery.

The resulting 'blank' then has its facets ground on a polishing lap, which usually takes the form of a horizontally-rotating disc with a surface and an abrasive powder appropriate to the hardness of the gem material (i.e. iron or copper with carborundum or emery powder, and a water lubricant). For the harder gemstones, such as sapphire and ruby, diamond dust (or a diamond compound consisting of diamond dust mixed with lanolin cream) may be used at this stage.

The gemstone is sometimes hand-held when grinding it into a blank, but in order to achieve more accurate control it is usually cemented into a holder called a *dop* when grinding the facets.

Finally, the gemstone, with all facets ground, but with their surfaces in a matt 'ground glass' condition, is thoroughly cleaned to remove any traces of coarse abrasive. The facets are then given a high-gloss polish on a leather or material-covered copper or wooden lap using a much softer abrasive such as cerium oxide or jeweller's rouge.

Are the facet positions and angles set entirely by eye?

Traditionally, lapidaries have ground and polished the facets on gemstones using the minimum of equipment. In many gem-producing countries, such as India and Sri Lanka, the grinding and polishing laps are still turned by hand, and the facets are ground by hand-holding the gem against the surface of the lap. Modern lapidary workshops, however, use electrically driven laps in conjunction with mechanical dops which enable the gemstone to be precisely indexed into the appropriate angles for grinding. Amateur lapidaries have tended to lead the way in the use of modern equipment and materials, as they have not been bound by the traditional and time-honoured methods of the industry.

What is meant by a 'native-cut' stone?

This is the term applied to a gemstone which has been polished by hand, usually in the country of origin. The term is often used to indicate that a stone has been cut for maximum weight or yield at the expense of its symmetry and correct proportions. Many such stones which are polished in the country of origin are re-cut in Europe to improve their proportions and value.

What type of equipment and techniques are used for polishing diamond?

All of the sawing and polishing techniques employed for diamond depend on the use of various grades of diamond dust as the cutting abrasive. Symmetrical or 'blocky' diamond crystals are usually parted in two by sawing parallel to and just above the line of the natural girdle to make a large and a small diamond.

The saw blade used to cut diamond is a specialised one and consists of a thin disc of phosphor bronze clamped between two support plates. The circumference of the disc is coated with diamond dust mixed with olive oil, and with the disc rotating at 5000 r.p.m., the diamond (which is secured in a solder dop) is lowered on to the cutting edge.

Sawing diamond is a slow process, and it may take several hours to part a one-carat diamond crystal in this manner. A quicker way to part a diamond is by cleaving. Unfortunately the cleaving planes in a diamond do not often lie in a direction which would result in the best yield from an octahedral crystal (*Fig. 6*).

However, cleaving is sometimes used to part larger diamonds which would otherwise take weeks or even months to saw in half. When this technique is used, the cleaver first of all scratches a groove or *kerf* in the surface of the diamond, using a fragment of diamond as the cutting tool. The cleaving blade is then inserted in the kerf and given a sharp tap to part the diamond in two.

Once the diamond has been sawn or cleaved, the individual halves are then *bruted* or *rondisted* to produce the round profile of the girdle. This is carried out by fixing the diamond in a dop, and rotating it at 1500 r.p.m. in a type of lathe. The corners of the stone are ground away to produce the round girdle by using another diamond as a cutting tool. This second diamond is mounted in the end of a stick, and is usually one of the sawn diamonds awaiting rondisting. Thus, while one diamond is being rounded off, the diamond used as the cutting tool is also having one of its corners removed, and will eventually be completely rounded off in the lathe.

Oval and marquise profiles are produced by rotating the diamond off-centre, and, as previously explained, these cuts will be used in conjunction with the natural shape of the diamond crystal to produce the best yield.

The next stage in the production of a finished diamond is *cross-cutting*, which involves the grinding of the large table facet, eight crown facets, eight pavilion facets and the culet. This is carried out on a cast iron lap called a *scaife*, which is rotated at 3000 r.p.m. and dressed with diamond dust mixed with castor oil (a thicker oil is used here because of the higher centrifugal forces acting on the diamond particles). The remaining group of 24 crown facets and 16 pavilion facets are then added, and each facet is given its final adamantine polish.

How are the facet angles adjusted when polishing a diamond?

In many instances this is done purely by eye, and depends on the skill of the polisher. The diamond being faceted is held in a dop which is secured by a copper stem to a weighted support called a *tang*. The angles of the facets are set by bending the copper stem.

Although both skill and a keen eye are necessary to set and check the grinding angles, the accuracy of the facet positioning is built up from a relatively simple symmetrical pattern. After positioning the large table facet, the polisher will grind two facets on exactly opposite sides of the table. Next, he will place two more facets between these, and then four more at the junctions of the first four (*Fig. 22*). Having established eight crown facets, he can then match these on the underside of the stone with a further eight pavilion facets. At each stage the angles of the crown and pavilion facets relative to the girdle are checked using a hand lens and an angle jig.

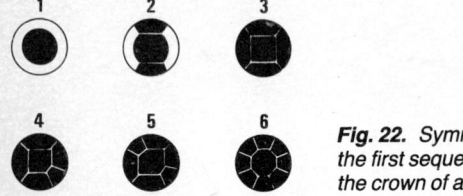

Fig. 22. *Symmetrical build-up of the first sequence of nine facets on the crown of a brilliant-cut diamond*

Modern semi-automatic dops contain an indexing mechanism which enables the main facet angles to be set precisely. Several fully-automatic polishing machines have also been developed which produce a sequence of up to 16 facets before requiring any operator attention.

8
Organic gems

Are organic gem materials still being created by living organisms?

Organic gem materials such as pearl, coral, ivory and tortoiseshell are still being 'manufactured' by living creatures, but gems such as amber and jet are fossilised substances and are becoming rarer as the various sources are slowly depleted.

What is amber?

Amber is a fossilised tree resin which was exuded from a particular species of pine tree over 30 million years ago. It is basically a hydrocarbon, and consists of a mixture of several different resins with succinic acid and oil. Over millions of years, the amber has become hardened to a point where its surface can be polished to produce a characteristic 'greasy' lustre.

What is the main source of amber?

Sea amber is found washed up on the shores of the Baltic, although small pieces of amber are sometimes deposited along the shoreline of the English east coast. Pit amber is mined principally on the Baltic coast near Palmnicken, which is now part of Russia.

What is meant by 'block' amber and 'pressed' amber?

Block amber is the name given to those pieces which are large enough for cutting into beads, cabochons and various other forms. Pressed or reconstructed amber, also known as 'ambroid', is made up from smaller pieces which are heated and compressed together to form larger pieces. Pressed amber can usually be recognised by the different areas of clarity and colour within the material, and by the presence of elongated air bubbles which have become trapped in the heat-softened material.

Another type of processed amber is produced from cloudy material by heating it in rape seed oil (colza oil). The heating process enables the oil to penetrate the fissures causing the cloudiness, and often results in the formation of stress patterns which appear as rounded spangles.

If amber is rubbed it will attract small fragments of tissue paper – is this a valid test for amber?

Amber certainly has the property of developing an electric charge when rubbed, and this results in it being able to pick up pieces of tissue paper. Unfortunately, several of its imitations also have this property.

What are the principal amber imitations?

Copal resin and Bakelite. Of these, copal, like amber, is a tree resin. However, unlike amber, copal is not fossilised but is a relatively 'young' and soft resin. Bakelite is one of the earliest of the plastics (a patent for the material was issued as long ago as 1906!) and was used extensively in post-Victorian jewellery as a substitute for amber.

How can amber be distinguished from its imitations?

With unmounted specimens, a specific gravity test will separate amber from Bakelite. If 10 level teaspoons of common salt are dissolved in a half-pint of water, this will produce a solution having a specific gravity of around 1.13. Amber, with an S.G. of 1.10, will float on this solution, but Bakelite (1.26) will sink. Unfortunately, copal resin has a similar S.G. to amber and cannot be separated from it by this test.

An identifying characteristic of copal resin is the readiness with which it crumbles under the pressure of a knife blade or a thumbnail. Broken surfaces of copal also show a network of fine cracks, and, unlike amber, copal can be softened or marked by the application of a drop of ether.

With faceted beads, and flat-based cabochons, it is sometimes possible to obtain a refractive index reading, that for amber being 1.54. Copal resin has a similar value, but the R.I. of Bakelite is much higher at 1.66.

Does the presence of a trapped insect indicate that the gem is genuine amber?

Not necessarily. Insects have been inserted into molten copal resin, and the product sold as amber. As the presence of insects in amber greatly enhances its value, it is important to make sure of the genuineness of the encapsulating gem material. It has been claimed that insects in amber always show signs of a struggle, as they were alive when trapped in the resin, whereas the insects inserted into copal resin were already dead! Insects have, however, been known to get trapped naturally in copal resin, so the best safeguard is to make sure that the 'tomb' is composed of amber.

Is jet similar to ebony in composition?

Only very remotely. Ebony is a hardwood, often used for carving, but jet, although somewhat similar in appearance, is a *fossilised* wood whose composition resembles that of lignite or brown coal. Its main source of supply used to be Whitby in Yorkshire, and although samples are still mined from this area, deposits are now worked in Spain, France and Utah in the USA.

Does jet have any imitations?

Vulcanite and 'Vauxhall' glass were two of the most widespread imitations used in Victorian jewellery. Vulcanite is a hard black vulcanised rubber, once used extensively as an electrical insulating material which was known as ebonite. Vauxhall glass, also known as 'French jet' and 'Paris jet', is a moulded black glass.

The best test for jet is a heated needle, which if pressed into the genuine material will produce fumes typical of burning coal, while vulcanite will smell strongly of burning rubber. Vauxhall glass feels much colder to the touch than jet, and often contains bubbles which are typical of glass of that period.

Are all pearls found in oysters?

Oysters are an edible species of mollusc and only very rarely produce pearls. The main source of pearls is the *Pinctada* sea-water mollusc, although some fresh-water pearls are produced by various clam and mussel species in Scottish and North American rivers.

How are pearls formed?

When a foreign substance, such as a grain of sand, enters the mollusc's shell, it acts as an irritant on the creature's soft flesh. The mollusc reacts by encapsulating the source of irritation with a skin or sac of a nacreous substance which is produced by the smooth inner layer of its shell (known as the *mantle*).

This nacreous substance consists principally of crystalline calcite within a very thin network of conchiolin cells. Even after the mollusc has completely covered the original source of the irritation, it will continue for several years to deposit successive layers of nacre, which eventually form a pearl.

If the pearl has grown in contact with the inner surface of the mollusc's shell, this will result in a *blister* pearl, but if it forms away from the mantle it will become a completely rounded *cyst* pearl.

The principal pearl fisheries are in the Persian Gulf and in the Gulf of Manaar (between the southern tip of India and Sri Lanka).

How are coloured pearls formed?

Coloured pearls are formed in the same way as the silvery-white varieties, but the colour has probably resulted from local differences in the sea-water environment. Pink pearls are found off the coast of Florida and in the Gulf of California in a mollusc called the 'great conch'. Black pearls are found in the Gulf of Mexico, and yellow pearls are a speciality of Shark Bay, Western Australia.

What is the difference between naturally-formed pearls and cultured pearls?

Cultured pearls are grown inside molluscs in the same way as natural pearls, but a high 'crop' percentage is ensured by the manual insertion of the source of irritation. The Japanese were the first to develop the technique of growing cultured pearls, which consists of inserting a mother-of-pearl bead (enclosed in a small fragment or 'graft' of mantle taken from another mollusc) into an incision cut in the shell of a mature three-year-old mollusc.

In a cultured pearl 'farm', the embryo molluscs (known as 'spat') are left to develop until they are big enough for seeding. After the beads and fragments of mantle have been inserted in the mature molluscs they are returned to the sea in cages. After three years, the molluscs are harvested and the cultured pearls extracted.

The earliest cultured pearls were produced by cementing the mother-of-pearl bead directly to the inner surface of the shell to produce a blister pearl (known as a 'Mabe' pearl).

A large fresh-water mollusc is used for culturing pearls around the shores of lake Biwa in Japan. This mollusc did not take to the bead nucleus method of culturing, and it was subsequently found that pearl growth could be initiated by simply inserting just the fragment of mantle into its shell.

Non-nucleated pearls of this type are known as *Biwa* pearls and are usually oval or baroque in shape. Because of the absence of the bead, they are also smaller in size and are often re-inserted as seeds into another clam to produce a crop of larger pearls. The size of the clam makes it possible for up to 10 pearls to be cultured at a time.

What are imitation pearls made of?

These are either solid glass spheres, mother-of-pearl spheres, or hollow glass spheres filled with wax. All three types are usually coated with a special preparation called *'essence d'orient'* to simulate the lustre of the real pearl.

How can natural pearls be distinguished from cultured pearls and imitation pearls?

It is relatively easy to identify imitations by inspecting the edges of the drill holes, as these will usually reveal chips in the coating and signs of the underlying glass surface. In the hollow variety, the filling of wax can be detected by inserting a needle into the drill hole.

Distinguishing between natural, or 'oriental', pearls and cultured pearls is more difficult. With nucleated types, inspection of the drill hole will usually reveal the sharp boundary between the bead nucleus and the outer coating of nacre, and within this boundary there will be a complete absence of growth lines.

As the mother-of-pearl nucleus in a cultured pearl has a greater specific gravity than the core of a natural pearl, this factor can be made use of in an S.G. test. A suitable test liquid can be made up from bromoform (diluted with monobromonaphthalene to an

S.G. of 2.71 – using a piece of Iceland spar as an indicator). The majority of natural pearls will float in this solution, while the majority of cultured pearls will sink.

Non-nucleated pearls are more difficult to detect, and modern testing methods for both these and nucleated pearls make use of X-ray techniques.

What is coral?

Coral is composed of a calcium carbonate (i.e. calcite) secretion from millions of minute marine polyp which live in colonies in shallow sub-tropical waters in the Mediterranean area, and in Malaysian and Japanese waters.

The coral used in jewellery ranges from the most expensive red variety to pink, pale pink, black and white. It can be distinguished from its glass, porcelain and plastic imitations by its cellular structure. Because it is a carbonate, the application of a small drop of dilute acid will cause it to effervesce.

Does all ivory come from elephant tusks?

The bulk of the world's supply of ivory comes from the tusks of the African and the Indian elephants (the latter producing the better quality material). However, sources of ivory also include the tusks of the walrus, the teeth of the hippopotamus, and even the tusks of fossilised mammoths.

Ivory, when viewed under the microscope, has wavy concentric growth lines (called *lines of Retzius*). These distinguish it from all its imitations, which include celluloid and bone (the latter containing canals which traverse the material and appear as a cellular structure end-on).

From what species of tortoise is tortoiseshell derived?

Despite its name, tortoiseshell is not obtained from the tortoise, but from the carapace or shell of the sea-going hawksbill turtle.

The best quality material comes from turtles found in the vicinity of the Moluccas and the island of Sulawesi in the East Indies.

Tortoiseshell imitations are mainly of plastic (in particular, casein). Unlike the individual small discs of pigment which make up the colour of genuine tortoiseshell (as seen under magnification), the pigmentation of the various plastic imitations is either evenly distributed, or can be seen as swirls of colour.

9
Gemstone simulants and synthetic gems

What is the difference between a gemstone simulant and a synthetic gem?

A gemstone simulant or imitation can be any material which has the same general appearance as the stone for which it substitutes (e.g. coloured glass, or a less expensive gemstone). A *synthetic* gemstone, however, must have exactly the same chemical composition, crystal structure and physical constants as its natural counterpart.

Are gemstone simulants difficult to detect?

Most simulants can be easily identified because their refractive indices, specific gravities and other characteristics are usually quite different from the gems they imitate. (The differences between the organic gems and their simulants are described in Chapter 8.)

Examples of gemstones which are sometimes used as simulants or substitutes for more expensive varieties are citrine (topaz), colourless sapphire and zircon (diamond), green tourmaline and green zircon (emerald), pyrope garnet, red spinel and red zircon (ruby), and blue zoisite (sapphire).

How many gemstones have been synthesised?

A large number of gemstones have been synthesised in various laboratories, but only the more successful and saleable of these have been marketed. Small gem-quality synthetic diamonds, for example, have been grown under laboratory conditions in America and Russia, but because of the high cost of the process, these have not so far been commercially viable, and are only of scientific interest.

Synthetic gemstones which have been successfully marketed include alexandrite, coral, emerald, lapis lazuli, opal, ruby, sapphire, spinel and turquoise. Among these, synthetic spinel is the exception as it is not produced as a substitute for natural spinel, but mainly as a low-cost simulant for diamond, sapphire and aquamarine.

There is also a group of synthetic gem materials which do not exist in nature, and are therefore more correctly described as 'man-made' rather than synthetic. These are mainly by-products of the laser and optical industries, and are manufactured as simulants for diamond. They include lithium niobate, strontium titanate, yttrium aluminium garnet (YAG), gadolinium gallium garnet (GGG) and cubic zirconium oxide.

Has the manufacture of synthetic gemstones affected the value of the natural gemstone?

The French scientist M. A. Verneuil began the commercial manufacture of synthetic rubies and sapphires in the early part of this century. Today, the Verneuil process is used world-wide for the production of synthetic ruby, sapphire and spinel with little or no effect on the value of the natural gemstone. The same is true of synthetic emerald, which began to be produced in quantity in America in the 1950s and in France in the 1960s.

How does the Verneuil process work?

Monsieur Verneuil spent most of his life perfecting the Verneuil furnace for the production of synthetic corundum. This furnace

(*Fig. 23*) is basically an inverted oxy-hydrogen burner which is used to melt alumina powder and to cause it to grow as a corundum crystal.

The high-purity alumina powder is fed in controlled amounts through the central oxygen feed pipe of the burner. As it passes through the hot region of the oxy-hydrogen flame, the powder melts and is collected on the surface of a ceramic pedestal. As

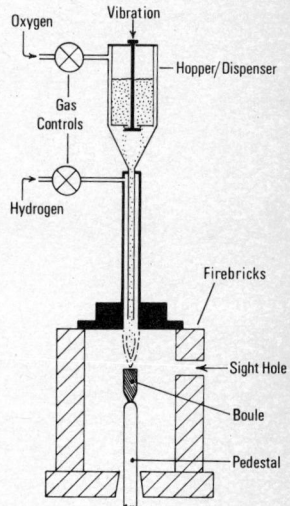

Fig. 23. In the Verneuil furnace, powdered source material is melted in an oxy-hydrogen flame to produce a synthetic crystal boule

soon as the molten powder begins to solidify, the powder feed rate is increased until a corundum *boule* begins to grow on the pedestal. As the boule increases in length, the pedestal is lowered so as to keep the top section of the crystal in the hottest part of the flame. Corundum boules of 15–25 mm diameter and 40–80 mm long take about four hours to grow, and weigh between 200 and 500 carats. The Verneuil process is also known as the *flame fusion* process.

How are the ruby and sapphire colour varieties of synthetic corundum produced?

To produce synthetic corundum boules having the various colours of ruby and sapphire, the appropriate colouring impurity is added to the alumina powder during its preparation. The additive or 'dopant' for ruby is chromic oxide, and for blue sapphire is titanium and iron oxides. Sapphires of other colours are obtained with nickel oxide (yellow), manganese (pink), copper (bluish-green), and cobalt (dark blue).

Is synthetic spinel produced in the same way?

Synthetic spinel boules are grown in the Verneuil furnace by using a powdered mixture of alumina and magnesia. It is interesting to note, however, that although natural spinels consist of a 1:1 chemical combination of alumina and magnesia, it has not been possible in practice to produce satisfactory crystals of synthetic spinel without increasing this ratio to 3:1. This has resulted in slightly higher values of R.I. and S.G. for synthetic spinel compared with those for the natural gem. Strictly speaking, the differences in chemical composition and constants of the man-made material should disqualify it from being called 'synthetic' spinel, but despite this the term 'synthetic spinel' has been universally adopted.

What other techniques are used to produce synthetic gemstones?

A variety of techniques (in addition to the flame fusion Verneuil method) have been developed, some of which were originally used to grow specialised crystals for the laser and optical industries.

Among the various techniques for gemstone production, the most important are the *flux melt*, the *hydrothermal* and the *skull crucible*. The flux melt method uses a high melting point solvent, or flux, in which to dissolve the chemical constituents of the gem material to be synthesised. The flux solvent is contained in a heated platinum crucible, and as the chemically-rich gem solution floats upwards into the cooler area of the crucible it becomes supersaturated and precipitates out on to seed crystals suspended in the flux. This method effectively copies one of the natural crystal-forming processes which occur in the earth's crust.

Synthetic emerald crystals are grown in this way by dissolving beryllium and aluminium oxides (plus chromic oxide as the colouring agent) in a flux of lithium molybdate at 800°C. The seed crystals are cut from either natural or synthetic beryl, and may take up to 10 months to grow to sizeable crystals of emerald.

Synthetic ruby and spinel, as well as the man-made crystals YAG and GGG, are also grown by this method.

The hydrothermal method uses water as the solvent by raising its boiling point to around 400°C in a pressure vessel called an *autoclave* (thus reproducing yet another of the natural processes of gem formation in the earth). The bottom of the vessel is filled with the source material, and the resulting solution becomes supersaturated as it rises into the slightly cooler upper section of the autoclave, where it precipitates out on to seed crystals.

Colourless quartz crystals for the electronics industry are grown in this way, and the hydrothermal method is now being used to produce the amethyst variety of quartz (by the addition of iron oxide and subsequent nuclear irradiation). Some synthetic emeralds and rubies are also grown by this technique.

The skull crucible method (developed in Russia) is used to grow crystals of cubic zirconium oxide, which are then cut and polished as diamond simulants. The zirconia powder used to produce the cubic zirconium oxide crystals (or zirconia for short) has a very high melting point, and cannot be contained in the normal type of crucible. The skull crucible, which was especially developed for the production of zirconia, consists of an open-work structure of water-cooled pipes.

The zirconia powder is placed in the crucible and melted by means of radio-frequency heating from a surrounding copper coil. The bulk of the powder melts, except for a thin layer next to the water-cooled pipes. This layer then acts as a high-temperature skull-like crucible for the molten zirconia. When the crucible is allowed to cool, crystals of zirconia solidify out of the melt. Because zirconia is normally tetragonal, and only adopts the cubic crystal system at high temperatures, a stabiliser (e.g. calcium oxide or yttrium oxide) is added to the powder. This stabiliser maintains the material in the cubic system as it cools to room temperature, and makes it a more convincing simulant for diamond, which also belongs to the cubic crystal system.

Coloured zirconia crystals (i.e. purple, orange, lilac, red, golden brown and pale green) are produced by adding rare earth dopants to the zirconia powder.

How can synthetic gems be distinguished from the natural variety?

With some synthetic stones this is relatively easy. Synthetic spinel, for example, has an R.I. of 1.727 and an S.G. of 3.64, compared with 1.717 and 3.60, respectively, for the natural stone (the colour of synthetic spinel seldom matches that of the natural stone). Synthetic emeralds grown by the flux melt process have lower constants than the natural gem (R.I. of 1.560, 1.563, S.G. of 2.65, compared to 1.573, 1.579 and 2.71, respectively, for the natural emerald). In a heavy liquid made up to an S.G. of 2.65 (using rock crystal as an indicator) natural emeralds will sink, but flux melt synthetics will float slowly up and down within the liquid.

The identification of synthetic rubies and sapphires is a little more difficult because all of the measurable constants are identical to those of the natural gem. The two most positive means of identification are the presence of inclusions and the detection of growth lines or colour zoning.

Because the natural gem crystallised relatively slowly in the earth, it was often host to a multitude of minute particles and crystals, which were incorporated in the growing gem as *inclusions*. The synthetic gem was formed much more quickly, and at worst the flame fusion varieties contain a few bubbles and traces of unmelted powder.

Types of natural inclusions vary from 'feathers' (groups of tiny cavities resembling a finger-print) to crystals (sometimes in the form of rutile needles which are described as 'silk').

Growth lines and colour zoning can be seen in both flame fusion and naturally-occurring rubies and sapphires, and are

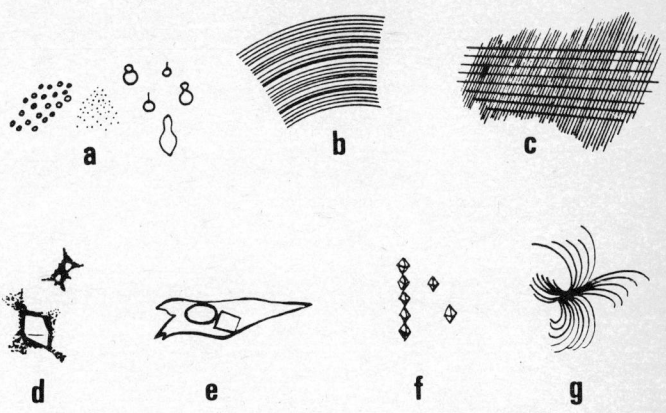

Fig. 24. *Typical inclusions seen in synthetic and natural gems: (a) and (b) powder and bubbles, and curved growth lines in flame fusion stones; (c) rutile needles (seen as 'silk' in natural rubies and sapphires); (d) zircon crystals surrounded by 'haloes' (seen in Sri Lankan rubies and sapphires); (e) a 'three-phase' inclusion, consisting of a void containing a liquid, a bubble and a crystal (seen in Colombian emeralds); (f) octahedral crystals (seen in natural spinels and sapphires); (g) 'horsetail' inclusion of asbestos fibres (seen in demantoid garnets)*

indicative of the way in which the crystal grew. In the synthetic gem, the growth lines and zones of colour (the latter especially noticeable in blue sapphire) are curved, while in the natural stone they follow the straight contours of the internal crystal formation. Some of the more easily recognisable inclusions are illustrated in Fig. 24.

What are composite gemstones?

These are gemstones which have been fabricated by cementing or fusing together two or three component parts. Except for opal doublets and triplets, these gems are manufactured for the purpose of deceiving the purchaser into believing that they are more expensive gems.

Opal doublets are made from a thin domed layer of precious opal cemented to a base of common opal or plastic. Opal triplets consist of a thin layer or veneer of precious opal cemented between a base and a quartz dome.

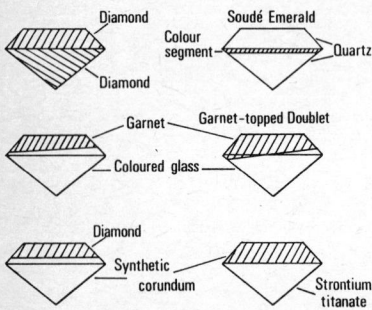

Fig. 25. *A selection of composite gemstones*

One of the most widely produced of the fake doublets (which is often seen in Victorian jewellery) is the garnet-topped doublet, or 'GTD' (*Fig. 25*). This consists of a top crown section of garnet fused to a coloured glass pavilion, and was made principally to imitate sapphire, emerald and ruby. GTDs are easily identified by the high R.I. of the table facet, by the presence of bubbles and colour swirls in the glass pavilion, and by signs of the join between the two halves (made more visible by immersing the stone in water).

Composite stones known as triplets have also been produced, the most well-known type being the *soudé* emerald which consists of a crown and a pavilion of colourless quartz or beryl, with a thin layer of green gelatine or sintered glass cemented or fused between them.

More rare (fortunately!) are the diamond doublets, which may consist of a crown and a pavilion of diamond cemented together (making a more valuable whole), or a crown of diamond cemented to a pavilion of synthetic white sapphire.

How can a diamond doublet or a diamond simulant be detected?

Diamond doublets can be identified by careful inspection of the stone for signs of a join in the girdle/crown area. The junction between the two halves may also be revealed by bubbles in the cement join, or by a reflection of the joining plane in the pavilion facets.

Diamond simulants (and doublets using a pavilion whose R.I. is less than that of diamond) can be detected by means of the 'tilt' or 'light spill' test, which is based on the total internal reflection of light from a brilliant-cut diamond. This test is made by looking into the crown facets of the stone, and then tilting the stone away from the line of viewing.

If the stone is a diamond, it will appear to be uniformly bright because its pavilion facets act as reflecting mirrors. This bright appearance will be maintained even when the stone is tilted so that it is being viewed at quite shallow angles to the table facet.

If the stone is a simulant, however, and has a lower R.I. than diamond, the rear pavilion facets furthest from the eye will begin to look black as the stone is tilted, because the light is 'leaking' out of these facets instead of being reflected back. The lower the R.I. of the simulant, the more marked will be the effect.

This test is only reliable for modern round brilliants cut to ideal proportions, and will not work for strontium titanate, which has an R.I. very close to that of diamond. However, this simulant is recognisable because of its excessive fire, which is over four times that of diamond.

If the suspect gemstone is unmounted, another simple check is to estimate its S.G. This can be done by comparing the stone's weight with its girdle diameter. The majority of diamond simulants are heavier than diamond, and (if cut in the ideal proportions) will weigh more for a given girdle diameter (*Table 5*).

Other more sophisticated tests include the use of a reflectivity meter (which identifies diamond by its high lustre), and the measurement of diamond's unusually high thermal conductivity by means of a diamond tester employing a heated test probe.

Table 5. Girdle diameters and weights of diamond and a diamond simulant

Girdle diameter (mm)	Zirconia simulant (carat weight)	Diamond (carat weight)
3.0	0.22	0.12
6.5	1.75	1.0
9.0	4.6	2.5

The traditional test of identifying diamond through its ability to scratch glass is not wholly reliable, as several diamond simulants also have this ability (e.g. colourless sapphire, YAG and zirconia). Diamond's extreme hardness does, however, help in its identification. If the crown facets of a diamond are inspected with a 10× hand lens, they will be seen to be perfectly flat and to have sharp well-defined edges. All diamond simulants are softer than diamond, and their facet edges will be less sharp. If the stone is a simulant, and has been worn for some years, it will usually show signs of damage in the form of scratch marks or chipped facet edges.

Appendix 1
Recommended further reading

Beginner's Guide to Gemmology, by P. G. Read, Newnes Technical Books, 1980.
An introduction to the science of gemstones, and a text for the Fellowship examinations of the Gemmological Association of Great Britain.

Diamonds, by Eric Bruton, NAG Press.
This book describes in well-illustrated detail the history, mining, polishing and marketing of diamonds.

Gemmological Instruments, by P. G. Read, Newnes-Butterworths, 1978.
A survey of modern gem test instruments, together with instructions on their use in the identification of gemstones.

Gems, 3rd ed., by Robert Webster, Newnes-Butterworths, 1975.
A comprehensive and detailed description of gemstones, including their occurrence, habit, characteristics and identification.

Gemstones for Everyman, by B. W. Anderson, Faber and Faber.
An ideal book for the non-professional, containing easy-to-read information on all aspects of precious stones.

Gemstones of the World, by W. Schumann, NAG Press.
Profusely illustrated with colour photographs, this book gives a brief but thorough description of the constants, characteristics and occurrence of the principal gemstones.

Gem Testing, 9th ed., by B. W. Anderson, Butterworths, 1980. This long-established work is a practical manual on gem identification, designed as an aid to distinguishing both natural and man-made gemstones.

Internal World of Gemstones, 2nd ed., by E. Gübelin, Newnes-Butterworths, 1979
Questions such as 'Genuine or fake?', 'What is that Stone?' are more easily answered with the help of this book. It gives advice and explanations as well as being stimulating reading.

Appendix 2
Gemstone constants

Gemstone	Approx. R.I.	D.R.	S.G.	H
Alexandrite – see Chrysoberyl				
Almandine (garnet)	1.77–1.81	–	3.8–4.2	7.5
Amazonite (feldspar)	1.53–1.54	0.008	2.56	6.0
Amber	1.54	–	1.05–1.10	2.5
Andalusite	1.63–1.64	0.01	3.18	7.5
Andradite (demantoid, melanite, topazolite-garnet)	1.89	–	3.85	6.5
Apatite	1.63–1.64	0.003	3.18–3.22	5.0
Aquamarine – see Beryl				
Benitoite	1.76–1.80	0.047	3.65–3.68	6.5
Beryl (aquamarine, emerald, goshenite, heliodor)	1.57–1.58	0.006	2.71	7.5–8.0
Bowenite	1.56	*	2.58	4.0
Chalcedony	1.53–1.54	*	2.58–2.64	6.5
Chrysoberyl (alexandrite, cymophane)	1.74–1.75	0.009	3.72	8.5

Gemstone	Approx. R.I.	D.R.	S.G.	H
Coral	–	*	2.6–2.7	3.5
Cordierite – see Iolite				
Corundum (ruby, sapphire)	1.76–1.77	0.008	4.0	9.0
Cubic zirconium oxide (zirconia)	2.09–2.18	–	5.54–6.0	8.5
Cymophane – see Chrysoberyl				
Danburite	1.63–1.64	0.006	3.0	7.0
Demantoid – see Andradite				
Diamond	2.42	–	3.52	10.0
Dichroite – see Iolite				
Diopside	1.67–1.70	0.03	3.3	5.0
Emerald – see Beryl				
Enstatite	1.66–1.67	0.01	3.25–3.30	5.5
Feldspar – see Amazonite, Labradorite, Moonstone, Oligoclase, Sunstone				
Fluorspar	1.43	–	3.18	4.0
Garnet – see Almandine, Andradite, Grossular, Pyrope, Spessartite, Uvarovite				
GGG	1.97	–	7.05	6.0
Goshenite – see Beryl				
Grossular (hessonite-garnet)	1.74	–	3.65	6.5

Gemstone	Approx. R.I.	D.R.	S.G.	H
Haematite	2.94–3.22	0.28	4.9–5.3	5.5–6.5
Heliodor – see Beryl				
Hessonite – see Grossular				
Hiddenite – see Spodumene				
Idocrase	1.70–1.72	0.005	3.32–3.42	6.5
Iolite (cordierite, dichroite)	1.54–1.55	0.008	2.57–2.61	7.5
Ivory (dentine)	1.54	–	1.70–2.00	2.0–3.0
Ivory (vegetable)	1.54	–	1.38–1.42	2.5
Jadeite	1.65–1.67	*	3.33	7.0
Jet	1.66	–	1.3	3.5
Kornerupine	1.67–1.68	0.013	3.28–3.35	6.5
Kunzite – see Spodumene				
Labradorite (feldspar)	1.56–1.57	0.01	2.7	6.0
Lapis lazuli	1.50	–	2.8	5.5
Lithium niobate	2.21–2.30	0.09	4.64	5.5
Malachite	1.66–1.91	0.25	3.8	4.0
Melanite – see Andradite				
Moldavite	1.50	–	2.53	5.5
Moonstone, orthoclase (feldspar)	1.52–1.53	0.006	2.57	6.0
Morganite	1.58–1.59	0.008	2.8	7.5
Nephrite	1.61	*	2.97	6.0
Obsidian	1.50	–	2.4	5.0
Oligoclase (feldspar)	1.53–1.54	0.007	2.64	6.0
Opal	1.45	–	2.1	6.0
Orthoclase (feldspar) – see Moonstone				
Pearl	1.52–1.66	–	2.71–2.74	3.5–4.0
Peridot	1.65–1.69	0.038	3.34	6.5

87

Gemstone	Approx. R.I.	D.R.	S.G.	H
Phenakite	1.65–1.67	0.016	2.95–2.97	7.5
Pyrite	–	–	4.84–5.10	6.5
Pyrope (garnet)	1.75–1.77	–	3.7–3.8	7.5
Quartz	1.54–1.55	0.009	2.65	7.0
Rhodochrosite	1.60–1.78	0.185	3.5–3.6	4.0
Rhodonite	1.73–1.74	0.012	3.6–3.7	6.0
Ruby – see Corundum				
Rutile	2.61–2.90	0.287	4.2–4.3	6.5
Sapphire – see Corundum				
Scapolite (blue)	1.54–1.56	0.016	2.60–2.71	6.0
Scapolite (pink, yellow)	1.56–1.58	0.02	2.60–2.71	6.0
Sinhalite	1.67–1.71	0.038	3.48	6.5
Smithsonite	1.62–1.85	0.23	4.35	5.0
Soapstone – see Steatite				
Sodalite	1.48	–	2.28	5.5–6.0
Spessartite (garnet)	1.80	–	4.16	7.0
Sphene – see Titanite				
Spinel (natural)	1.717	–	3.60	8.0
Spinel (synthetic)	1.727	–	3.64	8.0
Spodumene (hiddenite, kunzite)	1.66–1.68	0.015	3.18	7.0
Steatite (soapstone)	1.54–1.59	0.05	2.5–2.8	1.0+
Strontium titanate	2.41	–	5.13	5.5
Sunstone (feldspar)	1.53–1.54	0.009	2.64	6.0
Tanzanite – see Zoisite				
Titanite (sphene)	1.89–2.02	0.13	3.53	5.5
Topaz (brown/yellow)	1.63–1.64	0.008	3.53	8.0
Topaz (white/blue)	1.61–1.62	0.01	3.56	8.0
Topazolite – see Andradite				

Gemstone	Approx. R.I.	D.R.	S.G.	H
Tourmaline	1.62–1.64	0.018	3.01–3.11	7.0
Turquoise	1.61–1.65	*	2.6–2.8	6.0
Uvarovite (garnet)	1.87	–	3.77	7.5
YAG	1.83	–	4.58	8.5
Zircon (low-green)	1.78–1.84	–	3.9–4.1	6.0
Zircon (normal)	1.93–1.99	0.058	4.68	7.25
Zirconia – see Cubic zirconium oxide				
Zoisite (tanzanite – blue zoisite)	1.69–1.70	0.009	3.35	6.5

* Crypto-crystalline.

Appendix 3
Characteristics and occurrence of some gem materials

This appendix includes a series of brief 'profiles' which list the characteristics and occurrence of the more important of the gem materials. The gems are listed in descending order of hardness, starting with diamond.

Diamond

Chemical composition	Carbon
Crystal system	Cubic
Habit	Octahedron, dodecahedron, icosi tetrahedron (cubes rare), contact twin (flat triangular 'macle')
Lustre	Adamantine
Cleavage	Easy, parallel to octahedral faces
Varieties	Colourless and shades of yellow (Cape Series), brown and green (also rare 'fancy' shades of pink, orange, yellow, blue and green). Industrial diamonds are of poor colour and quality (boart, carbonardo and framasite)
Pleochroism	–
Occurrence	In volcanic pipes and secondary alluvial deposits. Historically in India, and then Brazil and South Africa and Russia. Important pipe mines in southern Africa are located in Angola, Botswana, the Republic of South Africa, Tanzania and

Zaire. Rich alluvial marine deposits along the coast of South West Africa (Namibia). Important pipes in Russia (Siberia)

Corundum

Chemical composition	Al_2O_3
Crystal system	Trigonal
Habit	Tapering barrel-shaped hexagonal bipyramids (sapphires). Also tabular hexagonal prisms, sometimes opaque in matrix of green zoisite (ruby)
Lustre	Vitreous
Cleavage	None, but parting parallel to basal pinachoid caused by lamellar twinning
Varieties	Sapphire (colourless, blue, green, yellow, pink, purple and orange). If unqualified, the name sapphire refers to the blue variety. Other varieties are identified by using the colour as a prefix (e.g. green sapphire) Ruby (red)
Pleochroism	Sapphire – Medium: blue, pale greenish-blue (none in yellow sapphire; in other colours, second ray has yellowish tinge) Ruby – Strong: red, yellowish-red
Occurrence	In crystalline limestone, or as alluvial pebbles Sapphire – Burma, Thailand, Cambodia, Sri Lanka, Kashmir, Australia, USA (Montana) Ruby – Burma, Thailand, Sri Lanka, Tanzania

Chrysoberyl

Chemical composition	$BeAl_2O_4$
Crystal system	Orthorhombic
Habit	Long prismatic crystals. Multiple inter-penetrant twins forming hexagonal star shape
Lustre	Vitreous
Cleavage	Imperfect
Varieties	Alexandrite (red in incandescent light, green in daylight)
	Cymophane (yellowish cat's eye)
	Chrysoberyl (green, yellow, brown)
Pleochroism	Alexandrite – Strong; green, yellowish, pink (in daylight), red, yellowish-red, green (in incandescent light)
	Cymophane and chrysoberyl – None
Occurrence	As alluvial pebbles
	Alexandrite – Historically in Russia. Main sources are now Sri Lanka and Zimbabwe
	Chrysoberyl and cymophane – Brazil, Burma and Sri Lanka

Spinel

Chemical composition	$MgAl_2O_4$
Crystal system	Cubic
Habit	Octahedron and spinel twin (contact-twin octahedra)
Lustre	Vitreous
Cleavage	Imperfect
Varieties	All colours including yellow. Colourless spinels are rare
Pleochroism	–
Occurrence	In metamorphic rocks and gravels Burma, Sri Lanka and Thailand

Topaz

Chemical composition	$Al_2(F,OH)_2SiO_4$
Crystal system	Orthorhombic
Habit	Flattened four-sided prisms with pyramidal or dome termination (prism faces striated along length)
Lustre	Vitreous
Cleavage	Perfect, parallel to basal pinachoid
Varieties	Colourless and shades of yellow to sherry brown
	Blue and blue-green
	Naturally-occurring pink stones are rare, but pink topaz can be produced by the heat treatment of brown and yellow stones
Pleochroism	Yellow – Medium: three shades of blue
	Blue – Weak: blue, pale pink, colourless
	Pink – Medium: pink, pale pink, colourless
Occurrence	In granite rocks, in pegmatites and as alluvial pebbles.
	Brazil, Sri Lanka, Russia and Burma

Beryl

Chemical composition	$Be_3Al_2(SiO_3)_6$
Crystal system	Hexagonal
Habit	Long hexagonal prism with basal pinachoid (other terminations rare)
Lustre	Vitreous
Cleavage	Imperfect, parallel to basal pinachoid
Varieties	Goshenite (colourless)
	Emerald (green)
	Aquamarine (pale blue or sea green)
	Heliodor (yellow)
	Morganite (pink)

Pleochroism	Emerald – Medium: green, yellowish-green
	Aquamarine – Medium: blue, colourless
	Heliodor – Weak: pale yellow, pale bluish-green
	Morganite – Medium: pink, bluish-pink
Occurrence	Emerald is found in metamorphic rocks such as limestone and marble. All other beryls occur in pegmatites such as coarse-grained rock
	Goshenite from USA
	Emeralds from Brazil, Colombia, India, Pakistan, Russia, Zimbabwe, South Africa
	Aquamarines from Brazil and the Malagasy Republic
	Heliodor from Namibia
	Morganite from Brazil, the Malagasy Republic, Zimbabwe and Namibia

Garnet group

Chemical composition	Pyrope	$Mg_3Al_2(SiO_4)_3$
	Almandine	$Fe_3Al_2(SiO_4)_3$
	Grossular	$Ca_3Al_2(SiO_4)_3$
	Andradite	$Ca_3Fe_2(SiO_4)_3$
	Spessartite	$Mn_3Al_2(SiO_4)_3$
	Uvarovite	$Ca_3Cr_2(SiO_4)_3$
Crystal system	Cubic	
Habit	Dodecahedron, icosi tetrahedron	
Lustre	Vitreous, except for grossular (greasy) and andradite (adamantine)	
Cleavage	None	
Species and varieties	Pyrope (blood red). Variety: rhodolite (rose red or pale violet)	
	Almandine (purplish-red)	

Grossular –
Varieties: hessonite (orange-brown, green, pink); massive grossular (jade green); hydrogrossular (jade green, 'Transvaal' jade)

Andradite –
Varieties: demantoid (green); topazolite (yellow); melanite (black)

Spessartite (orange, yellow, flame red)

Uvarovite (emerald green)

Pleochroism	–
Occurrence	As dodecahedron and icosi tetrahedron crystals in matrix
	Pyrope from Czechoslovakia, USA and South Africa
	Almandine from Czechoslovakia, Sri Lanka, the Malagasy Republic, Brazil and Australia
	Grossular from Canada, Russia, Sri Lanka (hessonite), South Africa (hydrogrossular), USA (hessonite) and Pakistan
	Andradite from Russia (demantoid), Switzerland (topazolite), Italy (topazolite)
	Spessartite from Sri Lanka, USA, Brazil, the Malagasy Republic
	Uvarovite from Russia, Finland, Poland, USA and Canada

Zircon

Chemical composition	$ZrSiO_4$
Crystal system	Tetragonal (amorphous in 'low' green zircons)
Habit	Four-sided prisms with bipyramidal terminations ('low' metamict types usually as pebbles)

Lustre	Adamantine ('normal'), vitreous ('low')
Cleavage	Imperfect
Varieties	Colourless, yellow, brown, orange, red, blue, green. Brown stones are heat treated in absence of oxygen to produce blue zircon, or in air to produce colourless, orange or golden-brown zircons
Pleochroism	Weak (except in blue); two shades of body colour
Occurrence	As alluvial pebbles, and as crystals in igneous rocks
	Sri Lanka, Cambodia, Burma, Thailand and Australia

Quartz

Chemical composition	SiO_2
Crystal system	Trigonal
Habit	Six-sided prisms with rhombohedral terminations, and fine lateral striations (except for rose quartz and the opaque quartzes, whose habit is massive)
Lustre	Vitreous
Cleavage	None
Varieties	Rock crystal (colourless)
	Amethyst (purple)
	Citrine (yellow, golden-brown)
	Rose quartz (pink)
	Smoky quartz (grey to brown)
	Prasiolite (green. Heat-treated Brazilian amethyst)
	Jasper (opaque red/brown)
	Aventurine quartz (opaque green or golden-brown, with spangles of mica)
	Quartz cat's eye (colourless, yellow-brown and green, with parallel fibres of hornblende or asbestos giving chatoyant effect)

	Tiger's eye (golden-yellow or golden-brown, containing parallel quartz channels resulting from pseudomorphic replacement of asbestos fibres, giving chatoyant effect)
Pleochroism	Hawk's eye (a blue variety of tiger's eye) Amethyst – Weak: purple, reddish-purple Citrine – Weak: yellow, pale yellow Non-existent to weak in all other varieties
Occurrence	In igneous rocks and cavities, and in alluvial geodes. Except for tiger's eye and hawk's eye, which come principally from South Africa, quartz deposits are world-wide. Best quality material from Brazil, Uruguay and the Malagasy Republic

Tourmaline

Chemical composition	Complex borosilicate of aluminium and alkalis, with various other metals
Crystal system	Trigonal
Habit	Long triangular prisms with rounded faces heavily striated along length. Sometimes terminated with trigonal pyramid
Lustre	Vitreous
Cleavage	None
Varieties	Achroite (colourless) Indicolite (blue) Schorl (black) Dravite (brown) Verdelite (green) Also pink, yellow and multi- or parti-coloured (along length of prism)

Pleochroism	Strong – All colours: two shades of body colour
Occurrence	In pegmatites, granite rocks and alluvial deposits
	Sri Lanka, the Malagasy Republic, Brazil, USA and Namibia

Jadeite

Chemical composition	$NaAlSi_2O_6$
Crystal system	Monoclinic
Habit	Massive
Lustre	Waxy
Cleavage	None
Varieties	Occurs in a wide range of colours and colour mixtures
	White, yellow, brown, green, mauve, black (like nephrite, it is a true jade material, but as translucent green 'Imperial Jade' it is more valuable than nephrite)
Pleochroism	None
Occurrence	Found in boulders or conglomerates, usually interlayered with serpentine. Also as secondary deposits in alluvial gravels
	Burma

Chalcedony

Chemical composition	SiO_2
Crystal system	Trigonal
Habit	Massive or botryoidal
Lustre	Vitreous
Cleavage	None

Varieties	The name 'chalcedony' covers all the crypto-crystalline quartzes
	The only varieties named chalcedony are the unbanded greys and blues
	Agate (in all colours with curved concentric bands)
	Onyx (black and white, straight banding)
	Cornelian (red and brown)
	Chrysoprase (apple green)
	Bloodstone/heliotrope (dark green with spots of red jasper)
Pleochroism	None
Occurrence	In cavities in volcanic rocks, or as nodules in sedimentary rocks
	Deposits are world-wide. Main deposits are in Brazil, India, the Malagasy republic and Uruguay

Peridot

Chemical composition	$(Mg,Fe)_2SiO_4$
Crystal system	Orthorhombic
Habit	Tabular crystals
Lustre	Vitreous
Cleavage	Imperfect
Varieties	Bright apple-green, olive green, brownish (rare)
Pleochroism	Medium: green, yellow-green
Occurrence	In cavities in peridotite rock, or gravels derived from them
	Also in serpentine deposits
	Isle of St. John in the Red Sea, Burma and USA (Hawaii)

Feldspar group

Chemical composition	Orthoclase and microcline $KAlSi_3O_8$
	Plagioclase $(Ca,Na)Al_2Si_2O_8$
Crystal system	Monoclinic (orthoclase)
	Triclinic (microcline and plagioclase)
Habit	Large prismatic crystals with well-defined 'blocky' structure
Lustre	Vitreous to pearly (moonstone)
Cleavage	Easy to perfect
Species and varieties	Orthoclase –
	Varieties: moonstone (translucent with adularescence); orthoclase (pale yellow)
	Microcline –
	Variety: amazonite (opaque green, blue-green)
	Plagioclase –
	Varieties: oligoclase (yellow); labradorite (multi-coloured iridescence); sunstone (gold spangled); aventurine feldspar (green with spangles); albite moonstone (yellowish translucent stone with chatoyance or asterism)
Pleochroism	None
Occurrence	In intrusive igneous rocks
	Orthoclase from Burma and the Malagasy Republic
	Moonstone from Sri Lanka, Burma, Brazil, India, Tanzania and USA
	Amazonite from USA, Namibia and Russia
	Oligoclase, sunstone and aventurine feldspar from USA, Canada, India and Russia

Labradorite from Canada, Australia, Russia and Finland ('spectrolite')

Nephrite

Chemical composition	Complex silicate of iron, magnesium and calcium
Crystal system	Monoclinic
Habit	Massive
Lustre	Greasy
Cleavage	None in large pieces, but each small crystal has perfect prismatic cleavage
Varieties	Green, white, yellow, but mainly a dark green
Pleochroism	None
Occurrence	In boulders and conglomerates, and interlayered with serpentine
	Also as alluvial pebbles
	China, New Zealand

Opal

Chemical composition	$SiO_2.n.H_2O$
Crystal system	Amorphous
Habit	Solidified veins in rock matrix
Lustre	Waxy
Cleavage	None
Varieties	Common or 'potch' opal (opaque without iridescence)
	Precious opals:
	White opal (whitish background with iridescence)
	Black opal (dark background with iridescence)
	Fire opal (translucent to transparent orange, occasionally with iridescence)

	Water opal (translucent to transparent colourless or brownish-yellow with adularescence)
Pleochroism	None
Occurrence	As solidified veins of silica gel in sandstone or clay matrix (precious opal), or in limonite matrix (common opal)
	Australia, Mexico (fire opal)

Turquoise

Chemical composition	A complex hydrated phosphate of copper and aluminium
Crystal system	Triclinic
Habit	Massive in rock veins and cavities
Lustre	Waxy
Cleavage	None
Varieties	Blue, blue-green and green, often banded or lined with traces of dark brown or black matrix
Pleochroism	None
Occurrence	As veins and nodules in limonite or sandstone matrix
	Iran (best quality blue), Tanzania, USA, Egypt (Sinai Peninsula), Australia, China

Pearl

Chemical composition	86% $CaCO_3$ (in form of aragonite crystals)
	12% conchiolin (organic material)
	2% H_2O
Crystal system	Orthorhombic (aragonite crystals)
Habit	Blister or cyst pearls

Lustre	Pearly 'orient' (natural pearls)
	Waxy (cultured, fresh-water and pink pearls)
Varieties	Oriental (white with iridescence)
	Pink (absence of pearly lustre)
	Black (black, bronze or greyish with iridescence)
Occurrence	Persian Gulf, coasts of Sri Lanka, Australia and Venezuela, Gulf of Mexico

Coral

Chemical composition	$CaCO_3$ (plus some organic material)
Crystal system	Trigonal
Habit	Branching plant-like structures
Lustre	Vitreous (in polished coral)
Varieties	White, black and blue
	'Noble' coral (pink and red)
Occurrence	In shallow sub-tropical waters
	Coast of Mediterranean, Bay of Biscay, coast of Japan

Amber

Chemical composition	Hydrocarbon. A fossil pine resin
Habit	Homogeneous drops or nodules
Lustre	Resinous
Varieties	Pale yellow, reddish-brown, greenish, bluish-violet, black
	Transparent to opaque
Occurrence	On the shores of the Baltic sea and the coast of Sicily
	Mined in Poland

Jet

Chemical composition	Lignite (brown coal). A fossilised wood
Lustre	Waxy
Varieties	Black, dark brown
Occurrence	England (Yorkshire), Spain, France, USA

Ivory

Chemical composition	Calcium phosphate. Organic
Lustre	Waxy
Varieties and sources	Dentine ivory from tusks of elephant, walrus, teeth of hippopotamus and tusks of fossilised mammoth. Also from front teeth of narwhal
	Vegetable ivory from hard white kernel of nut of certain palm trees in South America, and North and Central Africa

Index